Judaism

We offer our thanks to
G-d Almighty
who makes all things possible

Judaism

Compiled by

Levi S. Jacob

Ralphy E. Jhirad

Silverdale Books

ISBN : 1-85605-559-0

Published in 2000 by **Silverdale Books**
An imprint of **Bookmart Ltd.**
Registered No. 2372865
Trading as Bookmart Limited
Desford Road, Enderby
Leicester, LE9 5AD

© **Roli Books Pvt. Ltd., 2000**
Lustre Press Pvt. Ltd.
M-75, G.K. II Market, New Delhi-110048, India
Tel: (011) 6442271, 6462782, Fax: (011) 6467185
E-mail: roli@vsnl.com, Web site: rolibooks.com

Compiled by:
Levi S. Jacob
Ralphy E. Jhirad

Design by Inkspot

Printed and bound in Singapore

Page 2: "Even all the *Mitsvot* of the *Torah* cannot equal one word of *Torah*." (Yerushalmi Peah, 1:1)
Page 4: The sounding of the *Shofar* indicates: "Awake from your deep sleep you slumberers . . .
search your deeds, repent and remember your Creator . . . look into your souls, mend your ways
and deeds. Let each of you forsake his evil ways." (Rambam, Hilchot Teshuvah, 3)
Pages 8-9: "When will G-d build Jerusalem? When He will assemble the dispersed." (Talmud
Berachot, p. 49)
Page 10: "I shall give thanks to You for You have answered me and have become for me a
salvation." (Psalms, 118:21)

Contents

Acknowledgements

The compilers express their gratitude and appreciation to ORT India, Mumbai, The American Joint Distribution Committee, Mumbai, and to all those who extended a helping hand in compiling this book.

A special thanks to Mr Shimshon Tiefenbrunn for proof-reading the book to verify its religious accuracy.

To the following authors whose books have inspired the compilers to spread the message of Judaism:

Philip Birnabaum: *Encyclopedia of Jewish Concepts*

Rabbi Joseph Telushkin: *Jewish Literacy*

Isidore Fishman: *Introduction to Judaism*

Geoffrey Wigoder: *The Encyclopedia of Judaism*

Rabbi Wayne Dosick: *Living Judaism*

Rabbi Yaacov Vainstein: *The Cycle of Jewish Life*

Rabbi Dr Zalman Kossowsky: *The Modern Kosher Home*

Michael Fishbane: *Judaism*

Lisa Aiken: *To Be a Jewish Woman*

Chaim Pearl & Reuben Brookes: *A Guide to Jewish Knowledge*

Michael Kaniel: *A Guide to Jewish Art*

Rabbi Joseph Telushkin: *Jewish Wisdom*

To Roli Books Pvt. Ltd. for their respect for Judaism.

The publishers extend their appreciation to the Israel Government Press Office, New Delhi and the Ministry of Foreign Affairs of Israel for their generous help, and to Mr Ezekiel Isaac Malekar, Honorary Secretary of the Judah Hyam Synagogue, New Delhi.

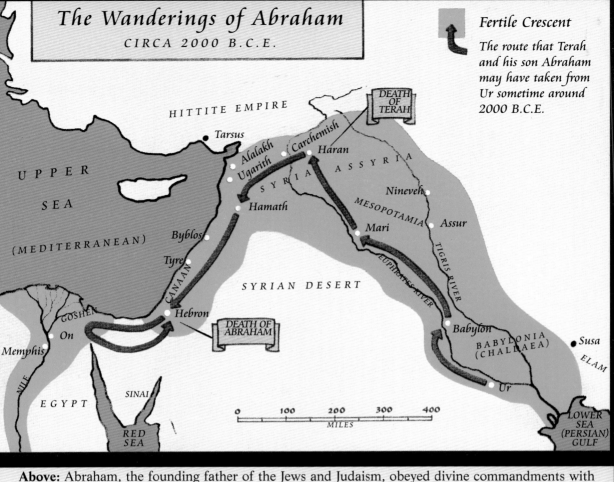

Above: Abraham, the founding father of the Jews and Judaism, obeyed divine commandments with total dedication. He was promised the land of Canaan as the home for the Jews.

Below: A commandment to remember the Exodus daily, is stated in the verse (Deuteronomy, 16:3): "You shall remember the day of your departure from the land of Egypt as long as you live." The *kiddush* recited on Sabbath eve notes that the Sabbath is a remembrance of the Exodus.

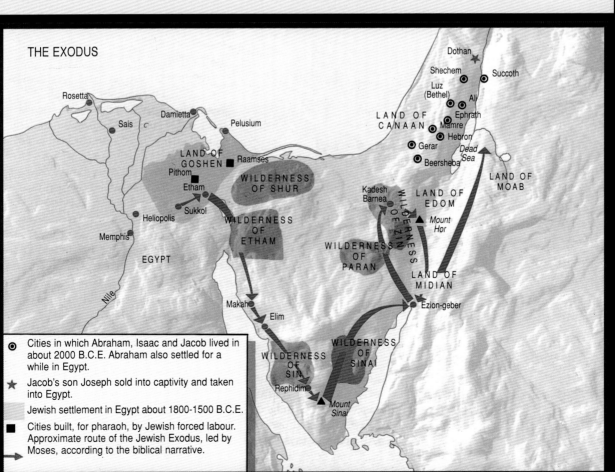

CHAPTER 1

Judaism: The Divine Faith

Words of Torah need each other. What one passage locks up the other discloses.

(BEMIDBAR RABBAH, 19:27)

It is a tree of life, to those
Who hold on to it, and those
Who support it are praiseworthy.
Its ways are ways of pleasantness
And all its paths are peace. (PROVERBS, 3:18)
For a good teaching I have given you;
Do not abandon My *Torah*. (PROVERBS, 4:2)

Judaism began about 4,000 years ago (18th century BCE), its origin going back to Abraham who was born in Ur in Babylonia (modern Iraq) during the Chaldean rule, his son Issac and grandson Jacob (also named Israel). Abraham was summoned by a Divine call and promised to move to Canaan to bring together a community of people with belief in one G-d. With this movement and settlement, a religious bond or covenant was established among Abraham, his descendants and his G-d. From the very start this covenantal bond and its ritual expression (circumcision of males) gave the people a self-conscious religious destiny. They were henceforth not solely part of the natural seed of Adam, the progenitor of humankind, but part of the divinely constituted seed of Abraham—the bearers of special promises about the settlement in the land of Canaan.

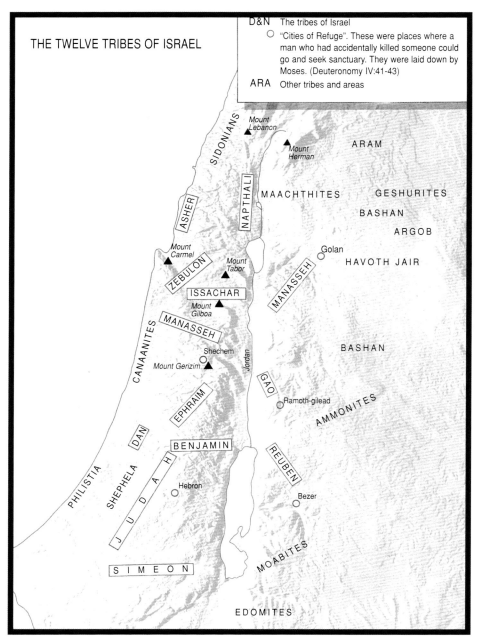

THE TWELVE TRIBES OF ISRAEL

D&N	The tribes of Israel
○	"Cities of Refuge". These were places where a man who had accidentally killed someone could go and seek sanctuary. They were laid down by Moses. (Deuteronomy IV:41-43)
ARA	Other tribes and areas

On a Holy Mission

The Exodus

It is only with the expansion of this covenant that all the multitudinous descendants of Abraham who came out of Egyptian bondage were led to freedom by Moses, who, according to the biblical narrative, was chosen by G-d to take his people out of Egypt and back to the land of Israel promised to their forefathers (13th—12th centuries BCE). The chosen people wandered for forty years in the desert of Sinai. It was there that they were forged into a nation and received the *Torah* (the manifestation of the will of G-d), which included the Ten Commandments and gave form and content to their monotheistic faith. With the *Torah* and its obligations, Israel and all of its descendants assumed their special spiritual destiny as a priestly kingdom and a holy nation. (Exodus, 19:6)

✡
Despite their single shared religious belief, the new Israelites preserved their original tribal structure which they traced back to the original
✡ patriarchs.

The Ten Commandments indicated the substance and scope of Israel's "priestly mission", but it did not provide for the specific duties and obligations that devolved upon the people as a "Holy Nation". These were developed in a series of revelations to Moses which he transmitted to the people and which, along with the Ten Commandments, finally became the *Torah*, commonly known as the Law, of which the Pentateuch is the written record.

After forty years, the children of Israel at last reached Canaan where the twelve tribes (corresponding to the twelve sons of Jacob) settled. They were governed by a series of prophets (religious sages who were endowed with a divine gift of revelation) till the time of the Prophet Samuel, when King Saul (1030 BCE) was chosen as the first king.

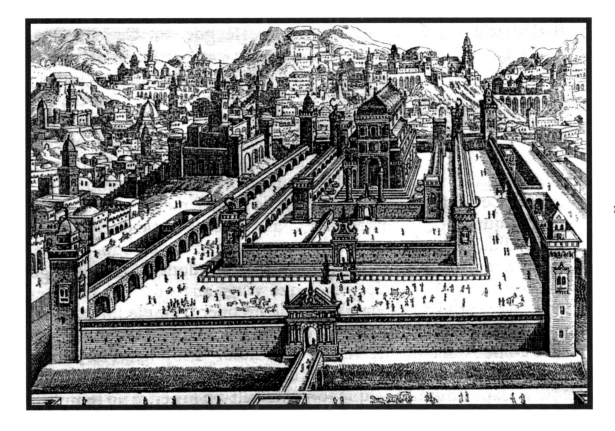

✡
"And behold, I intend to build a house to the name of the L-rd my G-d, as the L-rd spoke to David, my father, saying, 'Thy son, whom I will set upon thy throne in thy place, he shall build the house to my name.'"
(I Kings, 5:19)
✡

The First Temple

King David succeeded King Saul, united the twelve tribes into one kingdom and made Jerusalem his capital. He was succeeded by his son Solomon who further strengthened the kingdom by bringing in a period of stability and harmony to the land and the people. Crowning his achievements was the building of the Holy Temple in Jerusalem (950 BCE) as a centralisation of the worship of G-d; this became the centre of the Jewish people's national and religious life.

A Foundation of Three Pillars

Judaism is both faith and practice, a complete way of life, and reverence for life is its essence. Its tenets are based on the *Torah* of Moses, the revelation of G-d to Israel. The *Torah* teaches the fatherhood of G-d and the brotherhood of Man.

Judaism believes that a Messiah will usher in a Messianic Age. Between G-d and man there is no intermediary. No human being is free from sin or uniquely divine and the Gates of Heaven are open to man whenever he wishes to approach them.

Judaism is also a peoplehood of:

• shared history and destiny • shared language and literature • shared land and culture

G-d, Torah and Israel together form a three-pillared foundation. This is Judaism. It is this interdependence of religion and peoplehood that has sustained Judaism right through the generations; it is this link that is the guiding light of the Jews.

The *Torah*

The *Torah* is the embodiment of the Jewish faith. It is G-d's will communicated to mortal and finite man, directing him how to live.

The Holy Bible of Israel *(Tanakh)* consists of twenty-four books divided into three sections:

Torah - The Five Books of Moses: Genesis, Exodus, Leviticus, Numbers, Deuteronomy

Nevim - The Prophets

Kethuvim - Sacred Writings

Torah is faith, teaching, direction and above all, Law. For Jews, it is the Book of Word revealed to Israel and through Israel to all men. It includes doctrine and practice, religion and morals and is the source for the knowledge of the beginnings of Jewish thought and history.

The term '*Torah*' applies, in the first instance, to the Written Law, found in the Five Books of Moses. It also includes the Oral Law which is essential for applying the Written Law to everyday life.

The Written Law

The *Torah* relates the Jewish understanding of the creation of the universe and everything in it. It relates the encounter between Abraham and G-d that resulted in the covenant of faith. It recounts the revelation at Mt. Sinai when G-d began to give the commandments providing the moral values and standards of behaviour by which G-d wanted people to live. Along with the ethical commands, G-d gave Ritual Law, the instrumentality by which the ethical commandments are remembered and observed, and which serve to bring about a rhythmical order and enrich everyday existence by raising ordinary acts to the level of holiness.

To further enhance life, the *Torah* mandates the commemoration and celebration of special times and days, such as the Sabbath. Throughout the year, celebrations of holidays mark the seasons, commemorate historical events and sanctify time.

The *Torah* contains 613 *mitsvot* (commandments). The most famous of them are the Ten Commandments (sometimes known as the Decalogue; literally, "the ten Divine utterances/sayings"). Of the 613 commandments, 248 are positive: ("You shall . . .") and

the remaining 365 are negative commands: ("You shall not . . ."). There are two main categories of commandments in the *Torah*: ritual and ethical.

Ritual commandments revolve around ceremonies and rites of Jewish life such as observing the Sabbath and festivals, eating kosher food and participating in public worship.

Ethical commandments demand a certain standard of behaviour. Examples of ethical commandments are honouring parents, not stealing from others, not exploiting or using others for one's own advantage, feeding the hungry and dealing fairly and honestly in business. Throughout history, the prophets and the rabbis decreed laws to embellish and protect adherence to the *Torah*. These commandments of the rabbis had the same importance as the commandments of the *Torah* and were to be followed and obeyed with the same precision and sincerity.

In modern times, at least 200 of the 613 *Torah* commandments cannot be observed for they are concerned with the duties of the priests in the Holy Temple which was destroyed. However, both the ritual and ethical commandments form the basis for Jewish ethical and ritual conduct. THEY ARE THE LAWS BY WHICH JEWS ARE TO LIVE.

✡
"Whenever a man studies words of *Torah*, he is certain to find a meaning in them." (Talmud Eruvin, p. 54)
✡

Scribe checking a *Torah* scroll. This work requires careful observance of scribal law and proficiency in the use of a quill or a bamboo stylus.

The Oral Law: The Mishnah Gemara, Talmud and Shulkhan Arukh

As mentioned earlier, the Written Law was supplemented by oral teaching and interpretation, both derived from the divine revelation at Sinai. This teaching was for a long time handed down by word of mouth from generation to generation.

"Moses received the *Torah* from Sinai and handed it down to Joshua;

Joshua to the Elders;

Elders to the Prophets;

Prophets to the Men of the Great Assembly."

It was then passed from generation to generation by the leading rabbinic scholars who expounded the Oral Law until the time of Rabbi Yehudah HaNassi who edited the *Mishnah,* a detailed outline of Jewish Law (200 CE). Apart from *Halachah* (the guiding principle of law), the *Mishnah* contains a number of ethical and moral teachings intended to uphold man's dignity and sanctity. For almost 300 years after the *Mishnah* had been compiled, the Oral Law continued to be studied and developed by religious authorities.

Their commentary written in Aramaic is known as *Gemara* (completion), because it completes the *Mishnah.* The above two were embodied in one great encyclopaedia, the *Talmud,* in about 400 CE in Palestine and in about 500 CE in Babylonia. The *Talmud* is a compendium of Jewish lore and life: for in addition to the *Halachah* Laws, it contains the *Haggadah* (maxims, parables and anecdotes), which had been passed down through the centuries.

Both Palestine and Babylonia produced their own *Talmud*: the Palestinian *(Yerushalmi)* and the Babylonian *(Bavli) Talmud,* of which the latter has shaped the course of Jewish life upto the present day.

Several attempts have been made to excerpt the *Talmud* or to rearrange it so that it might be easier even for the less skilled to handle. Moses Maimonides (known as the Rambam) systematised the laws of the *Talmud* as *Mishneh Torah* (1200 CE). In 1600 CE, Rabbi Joseph Caro of Safed and Rabbi Moses Isserlis of Coracow (Poland) composed the *Shulkhan Arukh* (the "Table Arranged") in four volumes, comprising every aspect of Jewish Law, which has remained the standard authority for all Jewish law and practices.

This code is being continually brought up to date by the Responsa of the rabbinic authorities who have to decide with every change of condition how the immutable law of Judaism is to be applied.

"And you shall observe and do according to all that they teach you and according to the judgement they shall tell you, you shall do." (Deuteronomy, 17:10-11)

✡ Oral *Torah*—books of *Mishna* and *Talmud Bavli*. Rabbis identify wisdom with the *Torah*, for every branch of knowledge stems from the Tree of *Torah* revealed by G-d to Moses. ✡

The Jewish Concept of G-D

At the heart of Judaism is the belief in the Supreme Being who is omnipresent, all good and all powerful and who brought the world into existence and created man to worship Him. By doing so, man would share in G-d's goodness forever and be cast in His image. There can be no Jewish faith without G-d.

The first verse of the *Torah* clearly declares one of the main principles of Jewish faith. "In the beginning G-d created the heaven and the earth." G-d was the Creator and first cause of things.

G-d is central to Judaism and is always the One who establishes a covenant, who reveals the *Torah*, who requires obedience and sanctity, who guides people's destiny, and so on. This is particularly true of Judaism's central monotheistic proclamation of the *Shema: Hear O Israel, the L-rd our G-d, the L-rd is one; that G-d is one and unique.* As a result, the active religious life of a Jew is not one of theory and deduction, but one entirely filled with ritual and moral obligations, constantly making the reality of G-d present in the most personal and concrete terms.

Thus, belief in the absolute and indivisible unity of G-d is an important principle of the Jewish faith. He is perfect and complete in Himself. There is no other power besides Him or issuing from Him. G-d has no bodily form and whenever He is described in terms that could apply to human beings, it is only to satisfy our limited intelligence. The concept of one G-d and the declaration of His unity as contained in the *Shema,* remains a dominant feature and is recited loudly in the morning and evening prayers every day and also during a person's last moments on earth as an expression of confidence in His justice and mercy.

Fear of G-d

In many passages the Bible describes the good man as one who loves G-d and who fears Him. To fear G-d does not mean to be afraid of punishment He brings upon those who disobey Him. The Hebrew words "to fear" can and frequently mean "to be in awe of"—to have respect for.

To fear G-d is to experience a tremendous sense of unworthiness before the power and majesty of the Creator by contemplating the insignificance of man in the presence of his Maker—the Maker who is still concerned with man and desirous of his self-fulfilment.

✡ The concept of one G-d is contained in the *Shema* and is recited in the morning and evening prayers everyday. ✡

Love of G-d

Higher than the fear of G-d is the love of G-d. Is it possible to love G-d? We generally love things we can see or touch, things which are tangible, concrete things we can experience with our senses. In Judaism, the love of G-d is interpreted as submitting to His will, obeying His commands and helping to fulfil His purpose. In what manner can man obey G-d's will? Where is the record of that will to be found? Judaism replies that the *Torah* is the revelation of G-d's will. The *Torah* does not encompass the Scriptures alone, but all the lofty teachings about the relationship between G-d and man contained in the rabbinic literature and in post-rabbinic works. It thus embraces the sum total of Jewish religious expression.

The Chosen People

The Jews are "the chosen people" consecrated to G-d's service. To many it seems scandalous that a community should look upon itself as being singled out, superior and great. In reality, just the opposite is true.

The concept of "chosen people" does not mean that the Jews were chosen for a special privilege; in actuality, they were "chosen" for a sacred responsibility: to be a "light unto the nations" (Isaiah, 42:6; 49:6), a holy community reflecting G-d's light of love and law. The sacred Jewish responsibility is to receive, learn, live and teach G-d's word and will.

Jews and Judaism are called by a number of names. The first name-designation applied to Abraham and his descendants was Ivree, best translated as "Hebrew". In the Bible, the descendants of Abraham are called *Bene Israel*—"the children of Israel", or "the Israelites".

Israel is also the name given to the land of Canaan, the land that G-d promised to Abraham and his descendants, the land that became the Jewish homeland.

In biblical times, the ancient Jews were grouped according to twelve tribes, which originated from the sons and grandsons of the patriarch Jacob (the grandson of Abraham). Jacob's sons each received a fatherly blessing (Genesis, 49) and each became the progenitor of one of the tribes of Israel. These sons were Reuben, Simeon, Levi, Judah, Zebulun, Issachar, Dan, Gad, Asher, Naftali, Benjamin and Joseph. The names

✡
The Jews were "a chosen people" who held a sacred responsibility to be a "light unto the nations".
✡

Yehudi-Jew and Yahadut-Judaism come from the Hebrew word Yehudah-Judah, one of the twelve sons of Jacob.

During the sojourn in the desert led by Moses, the Tabernacle was built and the priesthood established; in fact, regular sacrificial worship began.

When the children of Israel entered the Promised Land, each tribe was assigned a geographical location. After the reign of King Solomon (931 BCE) when the kingdom split into two, ten of the tribes aligned together as the northern kingdom of Israel, and the other two tribes (Judah, Benjamin and a tiny remnant of Simeon) aligned as the southern kingdom of Judah.

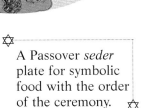

A Passover *seder* plate for symbolic food with the order of the ceremony.

In 722 BCE when Assyria defeated the kingdom of Israel, some of the inhabitants were sent into exile; others remained in the land and were assimilated into the conquering nation; still others made their way south to become part of Judah. The ten tribes of the northern kingdom disappeared. To this day, they are referred to as the Ten Lost Tribes.

The two remaining territorial tribes—the kingdom of Judah and those of the tribe of Levi made up the whole of the known Jewish community. That is why, till today, the people of the Chosen Land are known as the Jews and the religion is known as Judaism, respectively.

Ancestral Groupings

There were three ancestral groupings of the Jewish people, designated according to religious functions. They were Kohen, Levi and Israel.

- A Kohen is a descendant of the priestly tribe—the elite of the tribe of Levi—those who officiated at the sacrificial rites at the sanctuary and at the Holy Temple.
- A Levi is a descendant of the assistants to the priest.
- An Israel is any other member of the Jewish people, a descendant of neither a Kohen or a Levi.

The above designations were passed down from father to child.

Geographical Groupings

Since the Middle Ages, Jews have been designated into groups according to geographical areas:

Ashkenazim: Jews descending from the Jewish communities of Germany, Central Europe and Eastern Europe, including Poland and Russia.

Sephardim: Jews descending from the Jewish communities of Spain.

Edot HaMizrach: Jews coming from Persia, Yemen, Ethiopia and other eastern countries and are classified as neither Ashkenazic nor Sephardic.

Israel: The Promised Land

Eretz Israel has been central to Judaism since its very beginning. The covenant that G-d made with Abraham included the promise of an everlasting Jewish homeland which would be known as Israel: "Unto your seed I will give this land." (Genesis, 12:7)

The journey of the children of Israel through the desert had a clear destination. Joshua, the successor of Moses, was told by G-d, "Prepare to cross the Jordan (river) together with all these people, into the land which I am giving to the Children of Israel". (Joshua, 1:2)

When G-d spoke to Moses (Exodus, 3:8), He listed all the tribal inhabitants of the land. In precise detail, the land borders—north, south, east and west—were described by G-d to Moses (Numbers, 34:2-12). When G-d charged Joshua with the responsibility of bringing the people into the Promised Land, the boundaries were carefully set out by Him. (Joshua, 1:4-5)

Foreign invaders often invaded the land of Israel. In 586 BCE, the mighty Babylonians conquered the land, destroyed the First Temple built by King Solomon, brought an end to Jewish independence and sent the people into exile. In 538 BCE, the Persians defeated the Babylonians and permitted the Jews to return to Eretz Israel. It was there that the Second Temple was rebuilt.

In 70 CE, the Romans conquered the land, destroyed the Second Temple and sent the people into exile again—one that, this time, would last almost 1900 years. During that period of almost two millennia, Israel was ruled by different empires, but there was never one moment when some Jews did not live in the land.

The Jews outside the land always hoped and desired to return from exile to a restored and re-established Jewish homeland in Israel. In exile, they prayed facing Israel and Jerusalem.

The holiness of the land is due to the many laws in the *Torah* which apply to Eretz Israel and form the essential foundation of Judaism and the Jewish people.

Above: Yemenite Jewish woman. The Yemenite Jews belong to the group of Edot HaMizrach Jews.
Below: The Western Wall of the Temple destroyed by the Romans in 70 CE is a holy place for Jews.

The Western Wall

The remnant of the Western Wall of the Temple destroyed by the Romans in 70 CE became a holy place for Jews—the last vestige of the spot where the Holy Temple once stood.

Jews still come to worship there daily, weeping and lamenting over the destruction of the Temple and the exile of the people. Regarded with great affection as a reminder of a glorious past and a messianic future, the Wall became a symbol for the hope of restoration and return—that one day Israel would be re-established as an independent Jewish homeland and worship G-d at the site of the Holy Temple.

Jerusalem

The most important city of the Bible, Jerusalem has been the focal point of Jewish religious life and aspirations ever since David made it the City of David. It is the

site of both Holy Temples and Jewish pilgrims come at least three times each year to celebrate the festivals and offer sacrifices to G-d.

Jerusalem is so ingrained in Jewish life that for all the centuries, Jews in exile echoed the words of the biblical psalmist. "If I forget You, O Jerusalem, let my right hand wither." (Psalms, 37:5)

After its destruction in 70 CE, Jerusalem's role in national life diminished. It remained however, an embodiment of religious faith and spiritual glory. Jews have always wished to be buried on the Mount of Olives, believing that its proximity to the Temple mount would save them time and travail when Jerusalem would be restored and the dead resurrected.

As a city chosen by G-d (II Kings, 21:4; Psalms, 132:13), Jerusalem symbolised all of Judaism's most profound and sublime values and aspirations.

✡

"Why has G-d commanded that a blue thread be inserted in the fringes? Because it reminds us of Heaven." (Talmud Sotah, p. 17)

✡

Facing page: "If I forget thee, O Jerusalem, let my right hand forget her cunning." (Psalms, 137:5)

Pages 28-29: The priests, their head covered with prayer shawls, recite the priestly ✡ blessing at the Western Wall.

CHAPTER 2

Festivals, Holidays and Fasts

The four species naturally cause man joy by virtue of their beauty. G-d therefore commanded that these be taken during the Festival of Joy.

(SEFER HA CHINUCH)

Of the four species used in the Succoth ritual,
The citron has both taste and fragrance,
The myrtle has fragrance but no taste,
The *lulav* bears fruit which has taste, but no fragrance
And the willow branch has neither taste nor fragrance.
All four species must be taken together and absence
Of any one makes the commandment incomplete.

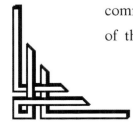 The Jewish calendar, accepted by Jews all over the world, is based on a lunar-solar system guaranteeing exact synchronisation of three fundamental divisions of time: the day, the lunar month and the solar year.

The need to use such a complicated system stems from the fact that the *Torah* commands take both the lunar month and the solar year into consideration. The months of the year are sanctified by the *Torah*: "At the beginning of your months you shall sacrifice a burnt offering to the L-rd . . . this is the burnt offering of each month of the months of the year" (Numbers, 28:11-14). Exodus, (12:2) tells us: "This month is for you . . .", and our sages said: "He showed him the moon in its renewal and said to him: when the moon is new that will be for you the beginning of the month." Therefore, the commandment is to determine and sanctify the months according to the renewal of the appearance of the moon. However, together with that, what has to be ascertained is that the month of *Nissan* will always be in Spring, as it is written: "Observe the month of Spring and keep the Passover to the L-rd your G-d." (Deuteronomy, 16:1). Thus there is the obligation to obviously consider the solar year as an additional basis for the calendar.

In order to bridge the gap between the lunar and solar years—a gap of approximately 11 days—the sages used the system of "Leap Year", by which one day is added to a month and a month to the year (*Adar II*) when it is necessary.

According to the Hebrew calendar, the year sometimes has twelve months, and is called a Simple Year (*Shanah Peshutah*); and at other times, the year has thirteen months (with *Adar II*) and is then called a Leap Year (*Shanah Me'uberet*—literally a "pregnant" year). In every cycle of nineteen years there are twelve Simple Years and seven Leap Years in a predetermined order.

"Full" and "Short" Months

Similarly, the Hebrew calendar has *full* months which have 30 days and *short* months with 29 days. The pattern is as follows: *Tishrei* is always full. *Tevet* is always short: from there on the months alternate—one full, one short. The exceptions to this rule are *Cheshvan* and *Kislev*—sometimes both are short and then the year is short (353 days); sometimes both are full and then the year is full (355 days); sometimes one is full and one is short and the year is normal.

The names of the months in the Hebrew calendar are of Babylonian origin, those returning from the Babylonian exile having brought them to the Land of Israel.

There are twelve Hebrew months. The table on p. 33 shows the months and their approximate equivalents on the secular calendar. In a leap year there are two months of *Adar*: *Adar I* and *Adar II*.

Rosh Chodesh

The first day of each Hebrew month is called *Rosh Chodesh*, the day when the new moon appears in the sky, starting its $29\frac{1}{2}$-day cycle of revolution around the earth.

The permanent calendar was fixed by Hillel II, a direct descendant of the famous Hillel, together with a number of rabbinical scholars about the year 359 CE. In the

Above: "If you have acquired knowledge, what do you lack? If you lack knowledge, what have you acquired?" (Midrash)
Page 30: Dancing and playing music are common features at Jewish weddings.

months that have thirty days, the thirtieth day is designated as *Rosh Chodesh* along with the first day of the new month. Since half of the thirtieth day technically belongs to the old month and the other half technically belongs to the new month, the whole thirtieth day is considered an "honorary part of the new month".

In the preceding centuries, the new moon and, hence, the first day of the month, could be determined only by careful observation of the sky. This was of great importance for ensuring that a festival occurring in any particular month should be observed at its proper time. As the *Mishnah Rosh HaShanah* (oral *Torah* related to *Rosh HaShanah*) explains, the new month was proclaimed as sanctified, on the evidence of witnesses claiming to have seen the new moon. These witnesses were thoroughly examined by the *Sanhedrin*—the highest court in Israel. This examination took place on the 30th day of the month. If the witness's testimony was accepted, that day was proclaimed as *Rosh Chodesh* and the previous month had only 29 days. If their testimony was not accepted or if no witnesses came forward, the following day was proclaimed *Rosh Chodesh* and the preceding month had 30 days.

Above: Man blowing a *Shofar.*
Left: The Jewish Calendar.
Of the creation of the sun and moon, the *Torah* states, "And they shall serve as signs for the set times—the days and the years" (Genesis, 1:14). Psalms, 104, 19 add, "He made the moon to mark the seasons".

MONTHS IN THE SECULAR CALENDAR

Tishri	September/October
Cheshvan	October/November
Kislev	November/December
Tevet	December/January
Shevat	January/February
Adar	February/March/April
Nissan	March/April
Iyar	April/May
Sivan	May/June
Tammuz	June/July
Av	July/August
Elul	August/September

On the day of *Rosh Chodesh*, special prayers are added to the synagogue service and a short *Torah* portion is read at the morning service in honour of the day. On the Sabbath preceding the week in which the new month will begin, a special prayer called the Blessing of the New Month, is recited in the synagogue, reminding the worshippers that the new month is approaching and they ask G-d for many blessings.

Rosh Chodesh is a *Yom Tov* for Jewish women—a special day, when they desist from the routine of the month to come together for study and celebration.

Jewish festivals bring together all the elements of Judaism's rich and resonant heritage. A Jewish holiday is called *Chag* (plural *Chagim*).

The Sabbath

The most important of all Jewish holidays—the central observance of Jewish life—is Sabbath. Sabbath is the once-a-week day of physical rest and spiritual rejuvenation on which the Jewish people emulate G-d who rested on the seventh day after the six days of creation.

The dedication of the fourth of the Ten Commandments to Sabbath is an indication of the importance of the Day of Rest to the Jewish faith. To the observant Jew the seventh day is holier than any other day. It is not merely a day when work is prohibited; it is a holy day that is filled with spiritual significance and meaning.

Sabbath dates back to the Creation. It is seen as a memorial to it and an acknowledgement of the existence of the Creator. The universe belongs to the Almighty and the world is given into the safekeeping of the human race for its use for six days. On the seventh day, it is returned to its rightful Owner. Work that is forbidden on Sabbath is anything that constructively interferes with the physical world G-d has created, such as lighting a fire, cutting flowers, using money . . . .

It begins, before sunset on Friday, when the woman of the house lights the candles. A short synagogue service at sundown begins the Sabbath, followed by the regular evening service, with certain insertions and changes for the Holy day.

Later at home, greetings are exchanged by saying "*Shabbath Shalom*—Sabbath Peace", followed by *Kiddush* (sanctification) and the taste of wine. In many homes, the

✡ Peace descends on a Jewish home every Sabbath. When a Jewish woman invites the Sabbath queen by kindling the lights at the proper time, her house is bathed in peace, holiness, warmth and unity. When the candles are lit and the Sabbath table set, the Divine presence ✡ blesses the house.

husband recites from the Book of Proverbs (31:10-31), "A Woman of Valour" in praise of his wife and the parents bless the children.

The prayer for bread, praising G-d who "brings forth bread from the earth", is recited over *challah*—a braided white or egg bread that is specially baked for Sabbath. This is followed by the evening meal shared by the whole family.

Following the meal, songs, chants and melodies are sung and the *Birkat Hamazon*—the prayer of thanks for the food that was eaten—is recited.

Sabbath morning is spent in the synagogue in prayers and worship and reading of the weekly *Torah* portion.

At home, the prayer of wine is recited, followed by the prayer for bread. The Sabbath afternoon service includes a short *Torah* reading of the new week's *Torah* portion. A third meal called the *Seoodah Shelishit*, is eaten.

Sabbath concludes approximately 45 minutes after sunset with the *Havdalah* service. This attractive ceremony separates the Sacred from the Profane, with the lighting of a candle, the fragrance of spices and the taste of wine.

The family members then greet each other by saying "*Shavuaa Tov*—May it be a good week". An additional fourth meal has been added by some, to prolong the holiness of the day and accompany the Sabbath Queen as she departs. This festive time is called *Melave Malka*.

Sabbath is also a memorial to the Exodus and the end of Israel's slavery in Egypt. The *Torah* does not just forbid work by the Jews, but also by servants or strangers or toiling animals that are "within his gates".

Annual Festivals

In addition to Sabbath, the *Torah* describes five major holidays:

Rosh HaShanah: The Jewish New Year

The Book of Leviticus instructs that on the first day of the seventh month (1st of *Tishri*), a day of rest will be observed: "proclaimed with the blast of horns".

This day has become known as *Rosh HaShanah*, the New Year, and the first of the Ten Days of Repentance, the period of spiritual self-examination that culminates in *Yom Kippur* (Day of Atonement).

The sound of the *Shofar* (ram's horn) is a call to penitence. It is integral to the *Rosh HaShanah* services, its sound being heard more than 100 times during the day's ceremonies.

Sacrifice of Isaac. This was the tenth and greatest of trials Abraham had to face, to prove that he was worthy of being the founder of the Jewish people.

Rosh HaShanah is also considered to be the anniversary of the Creation, particularly of the sixth day when man and woman were created. It is probable that it is also the anniversary of "the sacrifice of Issac", the supreme demonstration of Abraham's faith that has bound the Jewish people to the Creator. To test him, G-d called upon Abraham to sacrifice his son, Issac, but once Abraham had demonstrated his readiness to comply, the L-rd forbade the sacrifice and sent a ram as a substitute.

Yom Kippur: Day of Atonement

Yom Kippur is the day when the Almighty, after giving consideration to the deeds of every living being on *Rosh HaShanah*, finally passes judgement. The destiny of each individual in the coming year is fixed.

Yom Kippur was first established as the Day of Repentance for the Jewish people when Moses returned from Mount Sinai, carrying the second pair of stone tablets. He had learned that G-d had forgiven the Children of Israel for worshipping the golden calf—a sin which they had committed while Moses was receiving the original tablets inscribed with the Ten Commandments.

Yom Kippur is a day when all work, eating, drinking, washing, and so on, is forbidden—a day to be devoted only to prayer and supplication. The synagogue is the focal point, from the opening *Kol Nidrei* service to its close with *Ne'ilah* and the entire congregation is clothed in white.

This great Day of Awe lays stress upon self-examination, repentance and the need to focus on G-d. The liturgy is filled with the hope and confidence of Divine Mercy, but humbly so, and it is replete with extensive confessions and meditations, which are either read silently or aloud with the community. It is significant to note that an old ruling in the *Mishnah* emphasises that the prayers and rituals of *Yom Kippur* only atone for sins between the individual and G-d, not for sins between one person and another. For this reason it is customary to seek personal forgiveness or reconciliation from members of one's family and community before the beginning of the prayers. While *Yom Kippur* is observed once each year, the purpose and the spirit of *Yom Kippur* is observed each and every day. In the *amidah*—the silent meditation prayer that is recited by Jews three times each day—there is a prayer of repentance, a prayer seeking G-d's forgiveness for omission and transgression, thus making the individual understand that striving for self-improvement is a daily obligation.

The *succa's* roofing must allow visibility of the sky and must be constructed from materials growing on the earth.

Succot: The Feast of the Tabernacles

Closely following Yom Kippur, *Succot* is a festival of rejoicing that recalls the way in which the Almighty looked after the Children of Israel during the 40 years following the Exodus that they spent as nomads in the desert.

During this time a new generation grew up, born into freedom and motivated to build a Jewish homeland in the land the Almighty had promised to the Children of Israel.

The fragile *succa* (tabernacle or temporary dwelling) in which Jews spend time and eat meals during the seven days of *Succot*, recalls the vulnerability of the Children of Israel during their desert years and their total dependence upon the protection that G-d provided for them. Gratitude for survival is also reflected in the timing of *Succot* which begins on the 15th of *Tishri* and which coincided with the gathering of the final harvests of the year in the Land of Israel.

Another important element in the observance of *Succot* is the involvement in synagogue services of the four species bound together—a palm (*lulav*), myrtle (*hadas*), willow (*arava*) and a perfect citron (*etrog*). These four species have been compared to differences in the character of people. Those who have both knowledge and a good reputation can be compared to the citron,

Above: The four species are waved all round to acknowledge the omnipresence of G-d.
Below: The *succa* is a reminder to Man to remain humble and steadfast in his beliefs.

which has both taste and smell. Others resemble the palm which has neither taste nor smell, or the myrtle which has smell but no taste, or the willow which has taste but lacks a smell. Symbolically, bound together, the *lulav, hadas, arava* and *etrog* are strong because each compensates for any deficiency in the others.

Hoshana Rabba is the seventh day of *Succot*. Sharing several elements with the High Holidays, the special service is chanted in an austere and sublime melody with the cantor in solemn white garb. Other customs include seven processions in the synagogue and the beating of the willow branch at the end of the service.

Shemini Atzeret is observed on the eighth day of *Succot*. In Israel the eighth day is both *Shemini Atzeret* (The Eighth day of Solemn Assembly) and *Simhat Torah* (The Rejoicing of the Law). Outside Israel, the eighth day is *Shemini Atzeret* and the ninth day is celebrated as *Simhat Torah*—the Rejoicing of the Law. *Shemini Atzeret* is the day when the family leaves the *succa* and returns home. The use of the four species is discontinued on this day. Prayers for rain for the Land of Israel form part of the morning service.

Simhat Torah is the last day of the festival of *Succot*. It is the day when the annual cycle of the reading of the *Torah* in the synagogue is completed and the new cycle is begun.

The festival in Jerusalem during Temple times was a joyous, exhilarating occasion. As part of the modern festivities, the Scrolls of the Law are paraded seven times around the synagogue by the congregation and all males are called to read from the *Torah*. The man who reads the last portion of Deuteronomy is the "Bridegroom of the Torah", while he who reads the first portion of the Genesis is known as the "Bridegroom of Genesis".

Children play an important part in the festivities. They join in the procession and participate in the singing and dancing, usually with flags and miniature scrolls, thus adding to the gaiety and informality of the service.

Above: *Simhat Torah*. The scrolls are carried around in the synagogue.
Below: The *seder* service: Its purpose is to dramatically commemorate the Slavery and Exodus through symbols, ceremonies, special readings and hymns.

Pessah: A Celebration of Liberation

Pessah or Passover is a spring festival that commemorates the Exodus which took place 3,300 years ago, when the children of Israel followed Moses out of Egypt after 210 years of slavery. It is a seven-day festival beginning on the 15th of *Nissan*.

It begins with a *seder*, a family dinner, at which the story of the Exodus, as contained in the *Haggadah*, is retold and celebrated.

During the seven days of *Pessah* it is forbidden to eat leavened bread (made with yeast) and flat, unleavened *matzah* is substituted for it.

The ten plagues, which were imposed on the Pharaoh and his people to compel them to allow the Israelites to leave Egypt, are also made mention of in the story of the *Pessah* or Passover. The origin of the name of the festival is G-d's promise to "pass over" and spare the children of Israel from the plague of the slaying of the first born.

In biblical times, Passover coincided with the reaping of the first of the year's grain harvests— barley. On the second night of Passover, the

counting of the *Omer* (the days between the Passover and *Shavuot* holiday) begins, finishing 49 days later on the day before *Shavuot*.

Haggadah is the book used during the Passover *seder* which tells of the events of the Exodus from Egypt, and how to conduct the *seder* ritual. The book is filled with biblical quotations and rabbinic interpretations. There are now more than 2,500 separate editions of the *Haggadah,* reflecting the unique customs, ceremonies and concerns of the many and varied places and times in which Jews have lived. The *Haggadah* is one of Judaism's best known and most-loved books.

THE SARAJEVO
HAGGADAH

The *Haggadah* is the book used during Passover *seder*: it relates the story of the Exodus from Egypt and how to conduct the *seder* ritual.

Shavuot: The Feast of Weeks

This festival commemorates the momentous event when, just seven weeks after the departure from Egypt, the Ten Commandments were revealed to the Children of Israel.

Shavuot or "Weeks"—one of several names for this day—focuses on the time interval between *Pessah* and the day that Moses received the Law on Mount Sinai. This day is also known as *Zeman Matan Toratenu*—The Time of the Giving of the Law. Other names for *Shavuot* are agriculturally inspired. *Chag Habikurim* is derived from the traditional offering of the first fruits at the Temple and *Chag Hakatzir* relates to the harvesting of wheat, the last of the year's grain crops.

Shavuot marks the end of the seven weeks of the counting of the *Omer*. It has become customary to eat at least one full dairy meal during *Shavuot*. Tradition says this is because the dietary laws given to Moses and passed on by him orally, were not fully understood, so the people decided that eating an all-dairy meal would be the surest way to ensure compliance with the new *Kashrut* laws. Another view relates the dairy meal to a celebration of the biblical description—"a land flowing with milk and honey".

Festival Prayer Books

A prayer book used for a festival is called a *machzor,* which means "return" or "cycle". The "cycle" refers to the fact that each festival occurs once each year—thereby, relating to the "return" of the celebration of the festival.

Seven weeks after the Jewish people departed from Egypt, Moses received the Ten Commandments on Mount Sinai.

41

The *Hanukah* lights, lit in the synagogue as well as in each private home, publicise the miracle of the victory of the Maccabees against religious oppression.

Each important festival has one corresponding *machzor*: *Succot* (Tabernacles), *Pessah* (Passover) and *Shavuot* (Weeks, or Pentecost). The most famous *machzor* is the one used for the High Holidays: *Rosh HaShanah* and *Yom Kippur*.

All the festival *machzorim* (plural of *machzor*) contain the basic prayers. However, there are special changes and additions for each festival. For example, the High Holiday *machzor* contains the basic rubric of prayer, along with the special features for *Rosh HaShanah* and *Yom Kippur*. These mainly comprise special *piyyutim* (poems) reflecting the theme of the High Holidays. Since the High Holidays are the most commemorated of all Jewish festivals, the High Holiday *machzor*, with its meaningful prayers, is one of the most beloved of all Jewish books and one that all Jews are familiar with.

Holidays Commemorating Historical Events

Hanukah: The Festival of Lights

Hanukah, meaning "dedication", commemorates the completion of the purification and rededication of the Temple in Jerusalem, after its recapture by Jewish rebels led by Judah Maccabee, son of the high Priest Matithyahu.

Antiochus IV, the leader of the occupying Syrian/Greek Seleucids, had demanded that the Jewish people abandon their faith and turn to idolatry. This blasphemy, allied with his desecration of the Temple, ignited Jewish rebellion. In 164 BCE, with divine help, the outnumbered Jewish forces drove the invaders from Jerusalem.

The *Talmud* relates that the victors could find only one flask of the ritually pure oil required for the *menorah* (a candelabrum with seven branches) in the Temple and that this quantity was sufficient to keep the *menorah* alight for one day only. By a miracle, this single flask kept the flame burning throughout the eight days that were required to prepare new, pure oil. To recall the "miracle" of the oil burning for eight days instead of one, the holiday of *Hanukah* is celebrated for eight days at the synagogue and at home from the 25th of *Kislev*. On each evening, oil lamps (now candles) are lit in remembrance and gratitude. These are lit in a candelabrum known as a *Hanukiah*.

Two other *Hanukah* customs are eating doughnuts and playing with a *dreidel* (a children's spring top).

Purim: Feast of Lots

The message of this festival is the triumph of Good over Evil: the victory of Esther and her cousin Mordechai over the Persian courtier, Haman, whose aim was to destroy the Jews of the Empire.

Above: A prayer book for a festival.
Below: Lighting of *Hanukah* candles. Holidays and festivals are commemorated with lighting of candles and prayers.

The story is told in the Book of Esther. It begins when Ahasuarus, the Persian King, chose Esther as his new queen, unaware that she was Jewish. Later Mordechai learned of a plot against the king and was able to save him with the help of Esther. Finally, when Haman's intention of destroying the Jews became known, Esther convinced the King that he had been tricked into condoning the slaughter of his loyal Jewish subjects.

The King's reaction to the plot was to permit the Jews to defend themselves. As a result, on the fateful day, they were able to overcome their enemies. The day on which the Jewish people were supposed to be destroyed, the 13th of *Adar*, was chosen by the plotters after a draw of lots. It is for this reason that the festival is named *Purim*—Feast of Lots.

Haman begs forgiveness from Queen Esther.

Purim is celebrated with the reading of the scroll *(megillah)* of Esther and the telling of the *Purim* story on the 14th of *Adar*. It is customary for the children to dress up in a costume, the celebration including delicious refreshments of food and drink.

On *Purim*, it is customary to send little gifts of food and drink to family, neighbours and friends, and also to give food and monetary gifts to the poor and needy within the community.

Lag Ba'Omer

Literally, *Lag Ba'Omer* is the 33rd day of the seven-week period of the *Omer* that extends from Passover to *Shavuot*. In biblical times, this period coincided with the interval between the harvesting of barley—the first grain crop—and wheat, the last. To commemorate the terrible plague that decimated the great *Torah* seminary of Rabbi Akiva in the second century CE, the *Omer* has become a period of semi-mourning, when, for example, weddings are not permitted. The 33rd day on which the plague suddenly ended, provides a respite—a holiday for which there are no special rituals in the synagogue or traditional ceremonies at home.

It is generally celebrated out of doors and marked by lighting bonfires. These are seen as a direct link with the Jewish revolt against the Romans in 132-135 CE, which was led by Simon Bar Kokhba. During this brief period of freedom from Roman oppression, one of the first gestures of the Jews was to carry out a ritual that had, hitherto, been forbidden—the lighting of the signal fires communicating the declaration of *Rosh Chodesh*, the new lunar month.

Lag Ba'Omer is the only day during the *Omer* period when restrictions are eased so that, for example, couples can marry. Many believe that *Lag Ba'Omer* is also the anniversary of the death of Rabbi Simeon bar Yohai, the great scholar to whom authorship of the *Zohar* (the premier work on Jewish mysticism) is attributed. The Rabbi is believed to be buried in Meron so, on *Lag Ba'Omer*, there is a gathering in Safed, the home of the *Kabbalists* (the teachers of Jewish mysticism). The people then walk the eight kilometres through the mountains to Meron.

Tu Be-Shevat: New Year for Trees

The meaning of *Tu Be-Shevat* is the 15th day of the month of *Shevat*, a day, that for centuries, has been celebrated by Jewish people as the New Year for Trees. It falls in the January-February period when, in Israel, normally most of the winter rain would have fallen and the rising of sap brings life back to the trees.

The link with the Land of Israel provided by *Tu Be-Shevat* assumed new significance with the return of the Jewish people and the need to transform a desert into fertile land. It has become a national custom to plant trees on *Tu Be-Shevat*. The eating of fruit grown in Israel provides a symbolic link for Jewish people living abroad with their homeland.

In a traditional ceremony on *Tu Be-Shevat*, Sephardic Jews pronounce blessings over the Seven Species with which, according to the Bible, the Land of Israel is blessed: wheat, barley, grapes, pomegranates, figs, olives and dates.

Fast Days

The Fast of Gedaliah

The 3rd of *Tishri*, the day after *Rosh HaShanah* (two days after, in Israel) is the Fast of *Gedaliah*. The day recalls the assassination of Gedaliah, a member of a prominent Jewish family and a relative of King Zedekiah, who had been appointed by the Babylonian King

Nebuchadnezzar to be Governor of those Jewish people remaining in the Land of Israel after the majority had been sent away into exile. Gedaliah had based himself in the tribal lands of Benjamin and encouraged Jewish refugees from the Babylonian conquest to return. He divided the land left behind by the rich among the dispossessed.

His murder by Ishmael, an accomplice of the King of Ammon, provoked Nebuchadnezzar into exiling even more of the Jewish people from the Land of Israel. (Jews were allowed to return by the Persian King, Cyrus, after his defeat of the Babylonians in 538 BCE).

The Fast of the 10th of Tevet

This is a fast day that marks the anniversary of the beginning of the siege of Jerusalem by the Babylonians, a siege that culminated in the destruction of the Temple later in the same year—586 BCE.

The Fast of Esther

Facing page:
"When the ram's horn sounds long, they shall come up to the mount."
✡ (Exodus, 19:13)

This fast is observed on the 13th of *Adar*, the day before *Purim*. It recalls the fast by Queen Esther prior to her approach to her husband, the Persian King, to persuade him to foil Haman's plot to destroy the Jewish people.

The Fast of the 17th of Tammuz

This fast marks the day in 586 BCE when the walls of Jerusalem were breached for the first time by the invading Babylonian armies. Three weeks later the Temple was destroyed.

Tisha B'av

The 9th of *Av* is the bleakest day in the Jewish calendar. It is a day of fasting and mourning in memory of the destruction of both the first and the second Temple, the former by the Babylonians led by Nebuchadnezzar, the latter by the Romans led by Titus in 70 CE. The *Book of Lamentations* is read in the synagogue on *Tisha B'Av*.

CHAPTER 3

Prayer and worship

Let not thy prayer be a matter of fixed routine, but heartfelt supplication for mercy at the divine footstool.

(MISHNAH BERACHOT, 5:1)

What complaint can we make,
What can we say,
What can we speak, or
How can we justify ourselves?
We will search into our ways
And examine them and
Return to you, for your
Right hand is extended to
Receive all those who return.
(Morning service for Monday/Thursday)

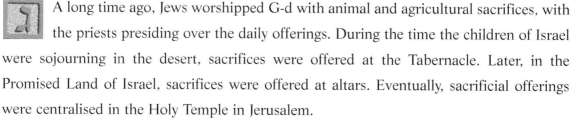

A long time ago, Jews worshipped G-d with animal and agricultural sacrifices, with the priests presiding over the daily offerings. During the time the children of Israel were sojourning in the desert, sacrifices were offered at the Tabernacle. Later, in the Promised Land of Israel, sacrifices were offered at altars. Eventually, sacrificial offerings were centralised in the Holy Temple in Jerusalem.

✡

Above: The *Siddur* Jewish prayer book.
Page 48: "And Issac sowed in that land, and found in the same year a hundred fold [*Heb-me'ah she'arim*]; and the L-rd blessed him."
✡ (Genesis, 26:12)

✡

Prayer timings for *Shabbat*, festivals and weekdays.

The popular connotation of "sacrifice" means giving up something to obtain a wish or to achieve something better. The animal and agricultural sacrifices offered for Jewish worship were for this purpose. The worshipper "gave up" an animal or grain, hoping to gain something of greater value: G-d's favour.

However in Hebrew the word "sacrifice" has a more significant meaning. Evolving from the Hebrew word *karov*, which means "to bring close", *korban* or sacrifice was meant to unite the worshipper into a close, intimate relationship with G-d. There were two communal offerings: one in the morning and one in the afternoon. The afternoon offering was smaller than the morning one, consisting of fine grain or meal. Additional offerings were made on festivals and the Sabbath to acknowledge that the day was special. Individual offerings were also made for special occasions or reasons.

In 586 BCE, the Holy Temple was destroyed and the Jewish people sent into exile: traditional animal sacrifices were replaced by prayers with words. This happened because the Holy Temple—where sacrifices were offered—was no longer in existence. In approximately 538 BCE, the Jews were given permission to return to the Land of Israel. About 20 years later, the Holy Temple was reconstructed and the practice of offering sacrifices was renewed. However, in addition to the offering of sacrifices, the Jewish people kept up the practice of reciting some of the prayers they had been used to saying during their period of exile.

Turning to Prayer

Prayers became much more important when the Second Holy Temple was destroyed and the people were sent into exile in 70 CE. As the exile became longer and longer, the prayers became more and more elaborate and ingrained and established in the life of the Jewish people. Prayers were substituted for sacrifices, and synagogues started replacing the Holy Temple.

The format for prayer was the same as the format of the sacrifices: there were two prayer services a day—the main service in the morning and a brief service in the afternoon. This was later supplemented by an evening service. It became obvious that human beings needed to seek out and communicate with G-d at different times throughout the day. On Sabbath and festival days, additional prayers were said to complement the additional sacrifices that were offered on these days.

Each prayer service developed its own character. Some of the prayers were taken directly from the Bible. Some were written by the rabbis and sages of the time. Each generation contributed its own prayers. Gradually, each prayer service developed a familiar pattern.

The agenda of the service began to be fixed, and this led to the development of the prayerbook—the *Siddur*.

The Siddur: The Jewish Prayer Book

The structured, organised collection of Jewish prayers recited on weekdays and the Sabbath comprises the *Siddur*. Meaning "order", a unanimously agreed upon order of prayers was fixed; they were formalised into the prayer book called the *Siddur*.

In 870 CE the first systematic *Siddur* was outlined by Rab Amram ben Sheshna Gaon in the Academy of Sura in Babylonia. A little over a decade later, the great Rabbi Saadya Gaon (882-942) compiled a more comprehensive *Siddur*. It is this *Siddur* which continues to serve as the basic format for Jewish prayer.

The basic *Siddur* is in Hebrew, but its words have been translated into almost every language of every country in which Jews have lived.

Through the years, the *Siddur* has been the organised vehicle by which a Jew could communicate with G-d. Its fixed structure provides a routine format of prayer; however, it is not rigid and remains open to accepting modern ideas and words which reflect the ethos of each generation and each individual. The *Siddur* serves as the model of the order of the prayer service until this day.

✡ Man must lose himself in prayer and forget his own existence. The gates of prayer are never closed. ✡

Berachah: Blessing

Blessings are the bases of communal worship service and it is through them that Jews acknowledge, praise, thank and petition G-d.

Maimonides, in his *Mishneh Torah,* divides the benedictions into three groups:

1. Blessings that express thanks to G-d for things we enjoy, such as eating and drinking;

2. Blessings which are recited before performing a commandment of G-d, thanking Him for the opportunity to fulfill a religious precept;

3.   Blessings of thanksgiving and praise, such as those recited during the early part of the morning prayer.

Birkat HaMazon: The Grace after a Meal

"Thou shall eat and be satisfied and bless the L-rd thy G-d." (Deuteronomy, 8:10)

The rabbis say that the above verse imposes the duty to say a blessing after a meal of bread. The rabbis originally composed three blessings:

1.   Thanking G-d for sustenance;
2.   Thanking G-d for inheritance of the Land of Israel and Torah;
3.   Blessing that Jerusalem should be rebuilt and the Temple service restored.

After the destruction of the Temple, a fourth blessing, containing the words "Who is good and does good", was added. This practice still continues till today. Ritual hand-washing was required before breaking of the bread.

✡ The religious discipline of Judaism demands washing of the hands on other occasions too, such as when getting up from bed or before offering daily prayers. ✡

The Synagogue

The Tabernacle in the wilderness and the Temple in Jerusalem were, before the Exile, the main centres of public worship, and symbolised the presence of G-d among the people. Priests offered the daily sacrifices on behalf of the community and it was only on special occasions that the individual took part in the service. During their exile in Babylon, the Jews came together for prayer and study, and on their return under Zerubbabel, and later under Ezra, they continued this practice. The House of Assembly became known as the *Beth Hakeneseth*. The *synagogue*—originally a Greek word also meaning House of Assembly—developed side by side with the Second Temple, and its services were arranged on the pattern of the sacrificial system.

In the synagogues today, several features serve as a reminder of the Tabernacle and the Temple.

1.   The *Holy Ark* represents the Holy of Holies, the innermost part of the Sanctuary and Temple, where even the High Priest can enter only on the Day of Atonement (Leviticus, 16:2). The Ark is built on the wall in the direction of Jerusalem, so that one prays facing the direction of the Temple's site.

2.   The continual lamp hanging before the Ark represents the lamp which burnt continually in the Sanctuary. (Exodus, 27:20)

3.   The *Sefer Torah* containing the Pentateuch is deposited in the Ark. It must be written in square Hebrew characters by a *sofer*—an expert and pious scribe—using black

The Talmudic sages praised group worship in the most elaborate terms: "A man's prayer is heard only in the synagogue—If a man is accustomed to attend synagogue and fails to come one day, G-d makes inquiry about him—When a man leaves the synagogue, he should not march with hasty steps; but when he goes to the synagogue, it is right to run." (Talmud Berachot, p. 6)

ink on specially prepared parchment. Over the breastplate hangs the pointer—it is used for the Reading of the *Torah*. The two rollers around which the scroll is wrapped are given the name of *The Tree of Life*—by which name the *Torah* is called. The gold and silver ornaments adorning the *Sefer Torah* remind us of the ornaments of the High Priest and are called sacred vessels.

4.   The *bimah* or platform was at one time used only for the Reading of the Law and for rabbinical discourses. In some synagogues, the Reader—known as the *Hazan* (representative of the Congregation)—leads the congregation in prayer from a place lower than the Ark. This custom is based on the verse: "Out of the depths have I called to You, O L-rd". (Psalms, 130:1)

5.   In obedience to the law contained in the Second Commandment, "You shall not make unto yourself any graven image nor any likeness . . .", no images or statues are permitted in the synagogue.

6.   Instrumental music was forbidden in synagogues on Sabbath and holy days by the rabbis; only in the Temple was music permitted on the days when sacrifices were offered. The absence of music is a reminder of the destruction of the Temple.

7.   Women are segregated from men, just as in the Temple times. The intention is to maintain propriety and decorum during the Service.

The association of the synagogue with education began in very early days. The elementary school was, for a long time, next door to the synagogue and so was the *Beth Hamidrash,* the school for higher learning. In time, the synagogue became the meeting place for students and scholars. Many synagogues today have a small room attached to them known as *Beth Hamidrash* where regular courses in rabbinic studies are conducted, especially on Sabbath days.

Worship Services

Jewish communication with G-d is built around three Jewish worship services every day of the year: one in the evening, one in the morning and one in the afternoon. The prayers are recited by traditional Jews either together in a synagogue, or in another communal setting or individually.

The evening service is called **Arvith**. The service gets its name from the Hebrew word *erev*—the root word of *Arvith*—which means "evening". It is the first service of a Jewish day since a Jewish day begins and ends at sunset.

The morning service is called **Shacharit**. The service gets its name from the Hebrew word *shachar* which means "dawn" or "morning". The service begins with a set of introductory prayers, which are known as *Birchot Hashachar*—the morning blessings— and *Pesuke Dezimrah*—the verses of song. Some of these blessings and prayers of praise to G-d are taken from the biblical Book of Psalms. They create the atmosphere and the tone for worship; they indicate the purpose of the worship service and serve as the transition from the "outside world" to the sanctuary.

✡ Worship services take place three times during the day: morning, afternoon and evening. ✡

The afternoon service is known as **Minchah**. The service derives its name from the Hebrew word *minchah,* which means "gift" or "offering". Though many Jews recite the *Minchah* and *Ma'ariv* services separately— *Minchah* at any time throughout the afternoon, and *Ma'ariv* much later, after dark, for practical purposes, both services are most often recited one after the other. *Minchah* is recited just before sunset, and *Ma'ariv* just after sunset, so that the worshippers come to the synagogue (or gather to pray) twice a day—once for *Shacharit* in the morning, and once for *Minchah* followed by *Ma'ariv* in the late afternoon or early evening.

A Jew can pray to G-d *(Daven)* either as an individual, or as part of a group. However, a group or quorum for public worship must consist of a minimum of ten people, thirteen years of age or older. The quorum is known as a *minyan.* Group worship can only be done at certain

55

✡
A minimum of ten
men, thirteen years
of age or older,
make up a quorum
✡ for public worship.

specific times—the three times allotted for daily worship, using the format of the prayer service.

Even during group synagogue worship, private prayers may be offered spontaneously when one wishes to communicate directly with G-d. If one is unable to attend the daily services at the synagogue, the prayers can be said at home. However certain prayers and public reading of the *Torah* are then omitted, since they can be recited only in a quorum of ten people.

Private prayers can be recited either at the traditionally set times, using the fixed words of the prayer book, or they can be offered anywhere, at any time, with the spontaneous outpouring of the mind and heart.

Keriat Ha Torah: The Torah Reading

The most important part of certain worship services during the course of each week is the reading of the Law. The *Torah* is divided into fifty-four separate sections or portions, each called a *parashah* or *sedrah*. One section is read each week (sometimes two); in this way the entire *Torah* is read from the beginning to the end in the span of one year, with the completion of the yearly *Torah*-reading cycle. The beginning of the new cycle takes place in the fall at the festival of *Simchat Torah*, at the end of *Succot*.

Torah reading is done four times each week. The first part of the allotted weekly portion is read for the first time on Saturday afternoon (at the Sabbath *minchah* service) and is repeated at the *Shacharit* service on Monday morning and on Thursday morning. The entire weekly portion is read at the Sabbath morning service.

Torah reading also takes place on all holiday and festival mornings, including *Chanukah* and *Rosh Chodesh*, and on fast days. The extract of the *Torah* read at each festival was specially selected by the sages for its thematic relationship and relevance to the holiday being celebrated.

After the *Torah* reading on Sabbath, *Rosh HaShanah*, *Yom Kippur* and festival mornings, and on *Yom Kippur* and other fast-day afternoons, a section from the biblical prophets is read out.

✡ A portion of the *Torah* is read each week. The entire *Torah* is read during the course of one year. ✡

Above: The Jewish home is the training ground for the teaching of the Jewish faith, traditions and values of the Jewish people.
Left: It is customary to touch the *mezuzah* with the hand upon leaving or entering the house, to express awareness of the fulfilling of the commandment and to show reliance upon G-d's protection.

CHAPTER 4

Code of Conduct

He who teaches his son is as if he had taught his son, his son's son and so on, to the end of all generations.

(TALMUD KIDDUSHIN, P. 30)

He who loves his wife as himself
Who honours her more than himself;
Who rears his children in the right path,
And who marries them off at
The proper time of their life;
Concerning him it is written,
"And thou wilt know that thy
Home is at peace." (TALMUD YEBAMOT, P. 62)

 Traditionally, the home is the nuclear holy space and the family, the nuclear ritual of Judaism. In the Jewish home is rooted the example for the kind of a life a Jew is expected to follow. It is in the Jewish home that the finest and noblest associations with Judaism are forged.

The home is the training ground for good habits and good deeds. In it are taught and exemplified the ideals of Jewish faith, the traditions and values of the Jewish people, the ideals of kindness, charity and hospitality.

A new Jewish house or apartment is first consecrated and dedicated as a Jewish home. To the doorpost at the right of entry, a *mezuzah* (a case with a Hebrew parchment on which the biblical *Shema* passage is inscribed) is affixed. The *mezuzah* is thus an external sign that the house is Jewish and a symbol of the Jewish values and behaviour espoused inside.

In the home, the dominant value is *Shalom Bait* ("the peace of the home") regulated by strong codes of parental respect and hierarchy.

Honouring Parents

In the *Torah* parents are equated with G-d; the duty to honour them in the same way as the Almighty Himself, is stated twice in the *Torah*. In the Decalogue, the commandment is: "Honour your father and mother that your days may be prolonged," (Exodus, 20:12) and in another book, "Ye shall fear every man his mother and father." (Leviticus, 19:3)

In fact the expressions "honour" and "fear" are found in the Bible only in reference to the Almighty and to parents. Reverence and respect for parents in the same way as given to G-d stems from the reality that parents, together with G-d, are responsible for bringing children into this world. Indeed life is the greatest gift given to mankind. It is in no way connected with worldly possessions, wisdom, or any other qualities possessed by parents. Honour and respect are due to every parent even if he commits serious misdeeds. (Yoreh Deah, 240:18) The *Talmud* (Talmud Nida, p. 31) puts it thus: "Man owes his creation to three partners: The Almighty, his father and his mother. His parents provide the physical matter and The Almighty, the soul, the spirit."

Maimonides (Hilchot Mamrim, 6:3) categorises the duties of children to their parents into two groups in keeping with "honour" and "fear" (or reverence) as they appear in the Bible. Revering parents—especially if they are old—entails attending lovingly to all their requirements for food and clothing; to stand up before them with the same respect that one would give to a teacher. Behavioural manifestations of fear or reverence are carried out by not sitting in their chairs; not contradicting them except by respectfully drawing attention to other information; not troubling them even in the face of a monetary loss; not calling them by their first names except if requested or wished for. The *Shulchan Aruch* (Yoreh Deah, 240) sets out the code of conduct towards parents in great detail; this is so because this was considered of extreme importance to family life, especially in its contribution towards achieving the highest standards of human society.

A child who abuses his parents brings divine wrath upon himself, as the *Torah* declares: "Cursed be he who curses his father and mother." (Deuteronomy, 27:16). A child should not hearken to his father when he tells him to transgress a precept of the *Torah*. If the son desires to go to some place to study the *Torah*, but the father does not give his consent for some reason, the son is not bound to listen to him since the study of the *Torah* is greater than the precept of respect to parents.

The *Torah* teaches the Jews to remember and honour their parents even after they have left this world. Mourning is observed for twelve months, during which time, the son recites *Kaddish*. *Yahrzeit* is observed by the children on the anniversary of death (according to the Hebrew date) in loving memory of their parents.

Tsedakah: Justice and Righteousness

Apart from justice and righteousness, *Tsedakah* is also the Jewish interpretation of charity. The living, the poor, the needy and the disabled are given charity in the form of alms; interest-free loans; help to earn a livelihood; sustenance to the aged, the sick, widows and orphans; providing education for poor children; helping out strangers ...

Giving charity to the poor is a biblical commandment: "If there be among you a needy man, one of your brethren . . . you shall not harden your heart . . . but you shall surely open your hand to him." (Dueteronomy, 15:7-8). It is recommended that one-tenth of one's income should be given as charity. No poor person should be turned away empty-handed, and *Tsedakah* should be given sympathetically. The best form of charity is when neither the giver nor the taker know each other's identity. The religious texts state that one should not insist on the repayment of a loan when the borrower is not yet able to repay, or to retain, for instance, overnight, a blanket given as a pledge, "for that is his only covering for his skin, wherein shall he sleep?" (Exodus, 22:24-26). On the other hand the borrower should not delay—he must return the loan as soon as he is able to do so. "Do not tell your neighbour, 'go and come back again and tomorrow I will give'." (Proverbs, 3:27:28)

✡ Jewish children are taught to honour their parents as much as G-d himself. The *Shulchan Aruch* sets out the code of conduct towards parents. ✡

Gemilut Chasadim: Acts of Loving Kindness

Gemilut Chesed is meant for all classes of society, be they rich or poor. This virtue can be practised by both the needy and the wealthy; it is also extended to the departed. *Gemilut Chesed* is an act performed in a completely selfless manner, the only

motivations being moral virtue and generosity of thought and action. Such acts include the following (Mishnah Peah, 1):

Hachanassat Orchim includes welcoming strangers in one's home and providing the hospitality of food and lodging. Any guest leaving the house should be escorted as this will give him a pleasant feeling.

Bikkur Cholim refers to the act of paying a visit to the sick to cheer them up with words of hope and encouragement; providing help to them wherever necessary and strengthening their faith in G-d.

Hachnassat Kalah means providing a poor bride with a dowry—this is a great *mitzvah,* especially where orphaned or very poor girls are concerned.

Halvayat Hamet refers to accompanying the dead to their last resting place, (Jacob's burial: Genesis, 49:29). Numerous Jewish communities have voluntary associations called *Chevra Kadisha*—holy groups whose members perform the sacred task of the last rites, which include washing the body, wrapping the shroud and supervising the funeral service.

Hava'at Shalom bein Adam L'chavero means making peace between man and his fellows; this is a cardinal religious duty enumerated in the religious texts. The search for peace between individuals and in society in general is strongly advised. The *Torah* prohibits harming one's neighbours in any way and preaches the preservation of peace and amicable relations among people. "Thou shalt not hate thy brother in thy heart." (Deuteronomy, 19:17). The commandment requires due respect for others' feelings, suggesting that any differences with one's neighbour should be pointed out with kindness and consideration. One should give fellowmen the benefit of the doubt and not be hasty in judging the motivation for their actions.

In Judaism, peace extends beyond the personal—it is a national ideal. A constant part of the daily prayers, it is also made mention of in the priestly blessing. Preserving peace between men is a sacred human duty. The rabbis call it the seal of the Almighty and one of the pillars of the world. The Jewish people greet each other with the word *Shalom* (peace). The prophets longed for the Messianic era of peace for all mankind.

The principal acts of *Gemilut Chesed* are enumerated in the Mishnah Peah (1:1): "The fruits of which man enjoys in this world while the stock remains for him in the world to come"; the "good heart" which prompts the performance of acts of kindness, distinguishes the pious Jews; "an act of charity, made without any ulterior motive, is of supreme Judaic value and obligatory on our people"; "three characteristics does the Jewish people possess; they are merciful, modest and perform deeds of kindness." (Talmud Yevamot, p. 79)

The Kosher Home

Since time immemorial the characteristic feature of the table in Jewish homes has been the dietary laws, stemming from the *Torah* which states their major rules. These are elaborated in detail in the *Talmud* and in later rabbinic sources.

The word kosher literally means "fit or proper" and describes those types of food which *Torah* Law declared fit to eat as well as the way in which these permissible foods were to be prepared.

The sages have taught that each Jewish home is like a "small sanctuary"—a dwelling place for the divine presence, and the table is likened to the altar in the sanctuary. In the sanctuary, utmost care has to be taken to see that, only that is offered which, according to *Torah* Law, is perfectly fit for the altar. Hence extreme care is required to see that only what is absolutely fit according to the dietary laws is brought to the table—the miniature altar, in order to ensure a home blessed with the divine presence and which truly serves as a small sanctuary.

The sages thus considered the Dietary Laws a vital aid in refining character and ennobling the soul. By prohibiting some foods and permitting others, Judaism aims at the health and welfare of man's body, without considering these precepts as sanitary regulations.

The purpose of the biblical injunction, "Thou shall not eat any abominable food," (Deuteronomy, 14:3), declares Nachamides, a Biblical commentator, "is to indicate that all things which are forbidden pollute man's pure soul . . . because forbidden foods being coarse, give rise to a denseness in the soul."

Kosher Animals

The *Torah* identifies kosher animals in different ways, depending on the species: mammals and fish are identified by physiological characteristics, while non-kosher birds are identified by name.

The animals which are kosher are quadrupeds that chew the cud and have split hooves: bovines, sheep, goats, deer, and the like fall into this category. Only those fish which have scales and fins are kosher.

The *Torah* identifies non-kosher birds by name. These are all birds of prey, including the vulture, falcon, owl and stork.

While the majority of birds are kosher, Jewish tradition dictates that one should eat only those birds which have traditionally been considered acceptable, like chicken, domesticated duck, geese, turkey and pigeons. All insects and creeping things are forbidden.

The laws of ritual slaughter are discussed in detail in the *Mishnah* and the *Talmud.* "Maimonides counts *Shechita* as one of the positive commandments of the Bible and quotes the *Talmud* in stating that 'Moses was instructed in the rules of ritual slaughter when he received the *Torah* on Mount Sinai'." (Talmud Hullin, p. 28)

Shechitah

All animals and birds must be slaughtered in an appropriate manner called *shechitah* in order to be kosher. Any animal or bird which dies a natural death or is killed in any manner whatsoever other than by *shechita* is non-kosher.

Shechita must be performed by a *shochet* who is certified by a duly authorised rabbi and approved of as having a good moral character and a mastery of the Laws of *shechita*.

It should be mentioned that the *Torah* was concerned with the sensitive treatment of animals. Kindness is the essence of the instruction: "Do not take the mother bird together with her young." (Deuteronomy, 22:6-7)

"The righteous man cares for the life of his beast, but the mercies of the wicked are cruel" (Proverbs, 12:10). This is the spiritual norm of Judaism. Care and kindness to animals are seen as vital factors in humanising man and are therefore included in the laws of Sabbath rest, as enumerated in the Ten Commandments. (Exodus, 20:10; Deuteronomy, 5:12).

Hunting is prohibited because it involves cruelty to animals. Torture or causing pain to any creature is strictly prohibited, hence the concern of Judaism that the slaughter of animals be painless and swift in order to prevent unnecessary suffering to the beast.

The *shochet* performs the ritual slaughtering by the swift movement of a highly sharpened knife thoroughly examined prior to slaughtering, and which cuts through in a fraction of a second and produces instantaneous unconsciousness in the animal. This method of slaughter causes maximum effusion of blood from the body. Following the slaughter, the *shochet* examines the knife for any nicks, and carefully examines the internal organs of the body for any signs of disease, injury or fracture which might render the animal or fowl unfit for human consumption.

Prohibition to Consume Blood

The starting point of the *kashruth* law is the severe prohibition of partaking of blood. The scripture states, "And ye shall eat no manner of blood, whether it be of fowl or of beast; whosoever it be that eateth any blood, that soul shall be cut off from his people." (Leviticus, 7:26-27; also Leviticus, 17:10-16). The verses of the Leviticus repeatedly prohibit the eating of blood, even while it is in the flesh; this is so because blood is the principal carrier of life and, hence, contains an element of holiness. Blood is sacred—the seat of life; therefore, it is not allowed to be used as food.

Moreover this instruction contains an ethical undertone: namely, to tame man's instincts of violence, making him different from savage beasts who delight in tearing other animals to pieces and are inflamed by the smell of their blood.

As a result kosher involves not only the species of the animal, but also the manner in which it is slaughtered and the manner in which the blood is removed from it before being eaten. The blood is removed by draining; this procedure is called *kashering*. The blood of fish is not included in the prohibition, hence, *kashering* the flesh of fish is unnecessary.

From Genesis, 9:4, the rabbis of the *Talmud* deduced one of the seven universal Laws, known as the Seven Noahide Laws: The prohibition of cutting flesh from the living animal, a barbarous practice common among primitive people. Life must altogether have departed from the animal before its flesh can be used "for the blood is the life." (Deuteronomy, 12:23).

The other six Noahide Laws are: prohibition of idolatry, murder, incest, robbery, blasphemy and the establishment of courts of justice.

Consumption of meat and milk

One of *kashruth's* fundamental principles is the prohibition of mixing meat and milk together. In this context milk includes all dairy products and prohibition of meat and milk thus also includes butter, cream, cheese and other dairy production as well. The *Torah* mentions the prohibition of cooking meat and milk together, three times. The law therefore postulates that there are three separate prohibitions:

• One may not cook meat and milk together even if not intended for human consumption, such as for pet food.

• It is neither permitted to eat meat and milk together, nor may products containing meat ingredients be eaten with products containing dairy ingredients.

"What is the service in the heart? The answer is 'Prayer'." (Taanit, 2)
"He who stands in prayer shall keep his eyes down and his heart upwards." (Talmud Yevamot, p. 105)

• Meat and milk which have been cooked together are not only prohibited as food, but one is not even allowed to sell them or derive any other benefit whatsoever from the mixture.

Foods that are neither of milk nor of meat origin—that is, fruits and vegetables are called *pareve* (neutral).

The same tablecloth or dishcloth may not be used to serve meat and milk. One is not allowed to serve meat and milk on the same table even in separate dishes and to two different people.

Meat may be eaten after milk if one first rinses one's mouth thoroughly. On no account, however, may one have milk after meat unless the prescribed period of time has elapsed in between. There are different traditions with regard to the time interval required. The most commonly accepted interval is that of six hours.

All fruits, vegetables and flour have to be carefully examined for worms, mites or other insects which must be removed before the produce can be eaten or cooked.

Utensils become disqualified if they have absorbed any food taste which might render them unfit as, for example, in the case of meat in a milk pot or vice versa. The *Torah* has clear guidelines as to which vessels can be restored to their previous use and the methods of doing so. Thus, as a general rule, earthenware vessels cannot be *kashered* but those made from metal, wood or glass can.

A *Mikveh*

A *mikveh* (literally "collection of water") is the ritual pool or bath. The *Torah* specifies a number of instances in which a person enters a state of ritual impurity. In order to re-enter a state of ritual purity, to be eligible to participate in the ritual rites, a person is to bathe— to immerse in natural flowing water as a symbolic act of purification. (Leviticus, 14:8, 15:5,9, 22:6 and Deuteronomy, 23:12). The act of immersion is called *tevilah*. The water is not used to remove physical uncleanliness, but serves as a symbolic rebirth. However, in a locale where there is no natural body of flowing water or in climates where the waters are frozen over for a part of the year, a *mikveh* is built. It is a pool-like structure to collect natural water from rain or snow and must be large enough for complete immersion. The waters of the *mikveh* are called *mayim chaim*—the waters of life—for *tevilah;* immersion in a *mikveh* engenders feelings of spiritual rebirth and rejuvenation. The *mikveh* is used by people before performing a sacred task, for example, by a scribe before writing a *Torah* scroll. It is also used by orthodox men before the Sabbath and by brides prior to their wedding as a symbolic act of purification and renewal. The most important use of the *mikveh* is by women observing the laws of family purity. Thus the *mikveh* is a vital component of every Jewish community.

CHAPTER 5

Rituals and Ceremonies

I will betroth you to me forever. I will betroth you to me for righteousness and justice and for kindness and compassion. I will betroth you to me for trust and you will know G-d.

(HOSEA, 2:21-22)

Man enters the world with closed
hands, as if to say:
"The world is mine;"
He leaves it with open hands,
As if to say,
"Behold I take nothing with me."
(KOHELET RABBA, 5:14)

 Upon awakening, the cycle of holiness is manifested in the form of rituals for the traditional Jew. The *halakha* regulates the initial ceremonies, as it does all others. The usual practice requires the male (after putting on a skullcap called *kipa* or *yarmulke)* to wash and recite prayers that emphasise the dependence of the human being on his Creator and how imperative it is to be respectful to Him at all times. One of these morning prayers, and often the first one young children are taught, states: "I give thanks to You, living and enduring King, who has restored me to my soul, with the great grace of Your trustworthiness. The beginning of wisdom is the fear of the L-rd . . . [whose] praise is everlasting." The service begins with a series of prayers that

praise the divine gift of knowledge, offer thanksgiving for daily sustenance and care, and emphasise the consciousness of Jewish identity and its obligations. These prayers may be recited alone or with a group at morning worship. As per tradition, the morning prayer service and all other worship services with a fixed time (in the *halakhic* category) are compulsory for males but not obligatory for women with household responsibilities.

All males, thirteen years and above, are required to pray three times daily, and to wear phylacteries during the morning service. These phylacteries, or *tefillin,* are ritual prayer boxes containing biblical quotations that are tied around the forehead and the left arm with leather straps. This ancient practice symbolises the biblical passages that recommend binding the teachings of G-d as a "sign upon your hand and frontlets between your eyes", and are a constant reminder of divine duties. The *tefillin* on the head now symbolises the obligation to serve G-d with one's mind and the one on the arm, near the heart, symbolises divine service with one's emotions. In early rabbinic times and through the Middle Ages especially, saintly persons wore the *tefillin* all day. Another practice for men entails wearing a prayer shawl called *tallit,* with special knots and fringes during the daily morning prayers. The Jews raise their shawls over their heads in prayer to indicate and facilitate personal devotion and concentration. Males also wear such fringes attached to a rope of undergarment, thus further fulfilling an ancient biblical injunction. The fringes are meant to aid one "to remember all the commandments".

✡

Page 68: It appears from *Talmudic* statements that the Sages did not walk four steps with uncovered head. (Sabbath, 118b; Kiddushin, 31a.) This was looked upon as a mark of reverence for G-d. (Sabbath, 156b) Man always needs a sign of his bond with G-d; on weekdays the sign is *Tefillin.* (Talmud Eruvin, p. 96)

✡

Morning Prayers

The first part of the morning prayers consists of biblical psalms and rabbinic prayers, based mainly on the themes of creation, revelation and redemption. The day thus begins on a historical and theological note, specifically one's dependence upon G-d and the obligations one owes G-d for his guidance and teachings. The affirmation of divine unity (the *Shema* prayer recited earlier) is an important part in this section of the service (and is recited again during the evening service). All prayers are a dedication to the principles of monotheism—the unity of G-d and all life under G-d. So important is this affirmation that it is customarily recited before sleep and as part of the death confession. It was also recited by Jews who died a martyr's death on account of these very principles.

The morning prayer service, as also every Jewish service, ends with a prayer called, in fact, The Prayer *(ha-Tefilla)*. The morning version comprises eighteen separate benedictions (fewer on the Sabbath) traditionally. These prayers start with praise and proceed to petition (for wisdom and health, for justice and peace, and for the restoration of the kingship of David and the ancient Temple service). The Prayer is recited silently while standing—it is, therefore, also called The Standing Prayer or *Amida*—and is repeated aloud by the prayer leader along with a number of verses recited by the whole community, proclaiming the divine sanctity. On Mondays and Thursdays (ancient market days), the portion allotted for the weekly *Torah* reading, is read out in an abbreviated form, so that all Jews might "fulfill the commandment" of *Torah* study in public. The service is concluded with prayers concerning personal requirements and wishes and collective redemption.

Breakfast is eaten only after morning prayers are over. All meals are preceded by a benediction over the food. Rabbinic *halakha* fixes blessings for other foods. After the meal, it is customary to say a number of prayers in thanksgiving to G-d "who sustains all life". As the day proceeds, special prayers can be said in celebration of the marvels of nature (like the wonder of a sunrise or sunset), reunions, partings and other human exchanges, and so on. In all these prayers the underlying theme is the constant awareness and realisation that life is a divine gift.

Apart from the routine daily and seasonal prayers, other occasions during the course of life are also singled out for ritual distinction. These occasions highlight or celebrate new beginnings and transitions from one stage of life to another.

✡ In the morning the *Amida* or Standing Prayer is recited silently by each individual. This is repeated by the prayer leader. ✡

Birth Rituals

Birth is naturally the first important moment in a person's individual and communal life. After a boy is born, a circumcision rite called a *brit* ("covenant", short for *brith milah,*— "covenant of circumcision") is performed eight days later. This ancient ceremony is symbolic of the transition of the infant from being a child of Adam to a member of the Jewish people. It is in this manner that the boy enters the "covenant of Abraham". The minor operation is carried out by a surgeon, called a *mohel*, who is specially trained for the job. Beginning with the mother, the child is passed among the relatives, and then handed over to the *mohel*. The *mohel* temporarily places the child on a "chair of Elijah". The boy is then held by the godfather (*sandek*) while the operation is performed, as per traditional custom. After the circumcision, the boy is handed over to his father or a special guest, while the *mohel* recites blessings in praise of G-d and for the welfare of the child. It is then that the boy's name is announced. The name given (for example, David, son of Abraham) will be how the boy will be "called up" when he is honoured to bless the *Torah* in later years; this very name will be marked upon his tombstone at death. The moment of fulfilment in the circumcision ceremony comes when the entire assembly exclaims: "Just as he has entered the covenant, so may he enter [the study of] *Torah*, the wedding canopy, and good deeds." This is how the life cycle is outlined, which the boy conforms to throughout his life.

There is another ritual associated with the birth of a male child: the *pidyon haben* (literally, "redemption of the [First-born] son"). Among the Jews, the first-born sons were consecrated to Divine service and were the original priests in the sanctuary until they were replaced by the Levites. (Numbers, 3:12). However, on the 31st day after the child's birth, the father could pay the priest five silver *shekels* (Numbers, 18:16) to release his son from these duties. Today, the silver *shekels* are replaced by coins to have the child released from this obligation.

The naming ceremony for a girl traditionally takes place in the synagogue during a Sabbath service after her birth, when her father is "called up" to read the *Torah*.

✡
G-d said to Abraham: "Throughout the generations, every male among you shall be circumcised at the age of eight days. Thus shall my covenant be marked in your flesh as an everlasting covenant." (Genesis, 17:10-13)
✡

Achieving Religious Majority

Boys start studying the *Torah* when they are about three to four years old; and, according to tradition, this event is inaugurated by making the child find and trace the letters of his name which have been covered with honey. This act is symbolic of the sweetness of life devoted to the *Torah* and the commandments. Though a boy is instructed in Hebrew and the traditional classics of Judaism from his youth, he does not become a formal member of the community until he is thirteen years of age. At that time, he becomes a *bar mitzvah,* literally, a "son of the commandment(s)". He is then allowed to perform all the *mitzvot* and is expected to do so with full responsibility for his religious behaviour. When the boy is first "called up" to the *Torah*, symbolic of his attainment of majority, his father intones a blessing commemorating this transition to adulthood.

Traditionally a girl achieves majority at the age of twelve, a time symbolic of reaching her menses. She is by then fully coached in whatever it takes to maintain a ritually correct home.

Commandments for Women

One of the fundamental obligations as Jews is to imitate G-d. Women were created with the potential of imitating G-d in the two greatest ways possible: by creating new life and by giving of themselves in the development and nurturing of others. Judaism values women's ability to bear, nurture and raise children. It also stresses how important it is for them to be stabilising forces in their husband's and children's development. From a Jewish perspective, should a woman choose to take on the challenge of having children, her job is not simply to be a "baby machine". Rather, it is to create and mould a Jewish body and soul who will carry on the mandate of perfecting the world in accordance with G-d's will.

✡ "... and you shall teach them to your children". (Deuteronomy, 6:6) This is a biblical precept. The moral and religious training of children is a command. It is a sacred obligation on parents as an essential part of the very heart of Jewish continuity. ✡

Of the 613 *mitzvot* in the *Torah*, women are only exempt from keeping seven that apply only to men. (There are other commandments that apply only to certain individuals or groups, such as priests, first-born males, Levites, kings, married men, and so forth). These seven are referred to as "time-bound positive *mitzvot*" and require Jews to say the *Shema* prayer, wear a *tefillin* and a fringed garment *(tsitzit)*, count the *Omer,* hear the blowing of the *Shofar* (ram's horn) on *Rosh HaShanah* (Jewish New Year), sit in the *succah* during the holiday of *Succot* (Tabernacles), and take a *lulav* (a palm branch bound with willow and myrtle) and *etrog* (citron) on the first day of the holiday of *Succot*.

Another reason that has been advanced as to why women are absolved from doing certain time-bound *mitzvot* is that this requirement would create tension for them. Although women are not obligated to marry or have children, Judaism recognises the likelihood that they will probably choose to do both. In order to facilitate these choices, the *Torah* does not obligate them to observe certain time-bound commandments. This is because married women's primary responsibilities, especially if they have children, are to their families and to their homes. Were they to have other responsibilities hanging over their heads, it would unfairly stress them.

Women are not obligated to attend prayer services in the synagogue. However,

women who do not have conflicting responsibilities to their families are encouraged to develop their connections with G-d through daily prayer, including attendance at a synagogue, if they so desire. They should also strive to give of their time, caring about and giving charity to others. For instance, if they have an income, they can give ten per cent of it to charity. They can similarly volunteer professional or free time to those who need such help or demonstrate their concern and comfort. In addition, they are encouraged to learn the *Torah* in a way that is relevant to them in order to

The Sages have said: "At thirteen years the age is reached for the fulfillment of the commandments" (Mishnah Avot, 5:21) This obligation has been termed in brief as *bar mitzvah*, literally, "Son of the commandment". *Tefillin* is closely associated with the spiritual maturity and adult conduct reached at the age of 13. (Orach Chayim, 60:37; Talmud Suca, p. 42)

fulfil their religious obligations properly.

Women are exempt from the obligation of studying the *Torah* for its own sake, unlike men who have to do so. The former are required to learn all the things they are required to perform or are forbidden to do. They must additionally study Jewish ethical works that teach how to develop proper ways of relating to G-d and other Jews.

Women should strive to pray the *Shemoneh Esrai* (18 benedictions) every morning and afternoon. When they cannot do this, they should at least pray in some form every day.

One of the *Torah*'s goals for men and women is to elevate the spheres of time, place (which includes objects) and persons to a higher spiritual level. Women have three special commandments: these are the *mitzvot* of keeping the laws of sexual holiness *(taharat hamishpachah)*, the separation of a piece of dough when they bake bread *(challah)*, and the lighting of the Sabbath candles. It has been suggested that each of these *mitzvot* taps into something special that women can uniquely contribute to the world. The *Torah* designates these *mitzvot* to women so that they will bring their spiritual influences into the material world.

Women have the ability and mission to bring G-dliness into their bodies and homes by observing their special *mitzot* and by using their inner reasoning to discern how to elevate the details of daily life to an overall holy way of life.

Judaism also believes that women were created to bring a number of qualities into this world. One of these qualities is modesty. The Jewish law and attitudes about modesty pertain to several areas of life. Both sexes are required to dress and comport themselves modestly and to speak in a refined and dignified way; however, the details differ as to what each should and should not do.

The laws of modesty require women to wear clothing that covers their arms down to the elbows, with necklines above the collarbone and with hems that reach below the knee joint. These areas must remain covered even when a woman is bending, reaching, sitting, and so on. The *Torah* requires married women to wear something that covers their hair. This is usually done by wearing a hat, a scarf or a wig.

It is an ancient Jewish custom not to go bareheaded especially during Service at the synagogue and for the recitation of blessings and prayers at home or elsewhere. The *Talmud* records (Talmud Shabbat, p. 118; Talmud Kiddushin, p. 31) that the sage Rav Huna, as a mark of Jewish piety, would not walk bareheaded for even four cubits. Rabbi Nachman's mother counselled her son: "Cover your head so that the reverence of Heaven be upon you." (Talmud Shabbat, p. 156). Although in Roman and later societies, covering the head was obligatory for servants as a stigma of their inferior status, the Jews wore a headcover as a sign of their being servants of G-d.

Thus, covering heads has become, since time immemorial, the Jewish way of showing reverence to G-d wherever any prayers are recited, or when studying the Bible, *Talmud* or other sacred books. Moreover, the pious Jew who recites many blessings during the course of the day, wears a skullcap, the *yarmulke* or *kippah,* during all his waking hours, both indoors or under the open skies, so that whenever G-d's name is mentioned, he does not find himself bareheaded. (Orach Chayim, 91)

✡ The *Torah* lays down special rules for women. These rules govern laws of modesty, behaviour and their role in life. ✡

Thus many laws of modesty govern how women should dress and comport themselves in the presence of men. However, the concept of modesty also applies to a woman's relationship with other women, as well as to her relationship with G-d.

The Wedding Ceremony

A wedding is a major moment of personal and social transition. The man and woman take their places

✡
The Sages regarded the wedding day as a day of judgement on which the bride and groom fasted to solicit the Almighty's blessings. It has been likened to a Day of Atonement for the bride and groom as it is said, "The sins of man are forgiven at marriage".
✡

under the canopy as productive communal citizens and fulfil the first *mitzvah* of the *Torah* to "be fruitful and multiply".

In *Talmudic* times, it was customary to go through a stage of "betrothal" *(kiddushin* or *erusin)* for some time before the "nuptials" *(nisu'in)*. The two stages were, however, combined in the post-*Talmudic* period and have since been celebrated together in the Jewish marriage ceremony. This wedding ceremony formally begins in the afternoon (the bridegroom and bride having separately returned from ritual ablutions, a traditional practice). The ancient contract formulas are reviewed by the "Arranger of *kiddushim*" and the document *(ketubhah)* is signed by witnesses. This *ketubhah* is read out at the ceremony itself, along with seven blessings extolling the beauty of creation and the joys of companionship. The bridegroom wears his white *kittel* and recites the traditional marriage vows: "You are betrothed to me, with this ring, in accordance with the laws of Moses and Israel." The couple shares wine and the groom breaks a glass. This is reminiscent of the sadness felt for the Temple's destruction even in moments of joy. Performing weddings at nightfall in view of the stars (which symbolise the divine promise to Abraham that his descendants would be as numerous as the stars), is considered a good omen *(mazel tov)*. Tuesday is also considered auspicious because of the phrase "and G-d saw that it was good". Marriages are avoided during certain periods associated with death or unfulfilment.

Praising the bride and entertaining the groom is considered to be a special *mitzvah*. Men and women dance in separate groups, and the bridegroom and bride are each hoisted up on chairs as the guests whirl round about. The wedding festivities are extended over a one-week period, beginning with the wedding day. During this week friends may invite the couple to a celebratory reception where the seven blessings of the marriage ceremony are recited by honoured guests. *Torah* teachings are given, and the *mitzvah* "to make the bridegroom rejoice in his bride" is fulfilled. Since the covenant at Sinai was already symbolised by the ancient rabbis as a wedding between G-d and Israel, with the *Torah* as the *ketubbah* and Moses, the go-between, "a deeper theological background is conveyed by the marriage occasion." There is a mystical aura to the event: the unity of the male and the female symbolises a more meaningful divine and cosmic harmony.

Revering the Dead

The important step of marriage is indirectly linked to the final stage of life, which is death. The white *kittel* that the groom first wears on his wedding day, later becomes his shroud. Similarly the prayer shawl *(tallit)* he receives at his marriage and which is often used to form the bridal canopy, is wrapped around him at death. The children born are the manifestation of a new family life; they are the continuing thread of social continuity after a parent's death and are obliged to mourn for the dead parent and look after the other. Finally, just as a special meal is provided after the circumcision and wedding ceremonies, so is it customary for a "meal of consolation" to be provided to the mourners by relatives and friends upon the return from the grave site, this custom symbolising social continuity.

The period between death and burial (usually within the same day) is the first step in the stage of transition. Upon hearing of the death of a relative, the mourner (now called *onen)* rips his or her garments and acknowledges G-d as "the true Judge". The *onen* is then required to follow certain restrictions: shaving, the wearing of leather and certain types of washing are forbidden. He or she spends time reciting psalms and is exempted from most positive commandments. The *onen* has to make sure that the deceased's body is ritually purified and clad in a shroud. "Watchers" stay awake with the corpse and recite psalms. The second stage of mourning begins after the burial ceremony and the first recitation of the *kaddish* prayer (a glorification of G-d's power and redemptive help). This stage called *shiva* ("seven" in Hebrew) lasts for seven days. From this time on the mourner is known as an *avel*. The close kins stay together at the home of the dead person during this week and customarily sit on low seats. During the daily prayers performed in the house of the mourner, certain prayers are deleted and psalms added. The rest of the community visits the bereaved and offers its condolences. This is considered an important *mitzvah*. Custom demands that a visitor does not begin any conversation with an *avel*, out of respect for the grief of the mourner; and if a conversation is started, it is restricted to the merits of the deceased. When taking leave from an *avel*, a visitor says in Hebrew: "May the Almighty comfort you, together with all the mourners of Zion and Jerusalem".

After *shiva,* the mourner returns to routine activities, though refraining from celebrations (even a haircut or wearing newly pressed clothes are forbidden) for thirty days. During this period (the third stage) too and for eleven months thereafter (the fourth stage), the *kaddish* is recited during communal services. Right through the third and fourth stages, the mourner does not sit in his or her customary seat in the synagogue. The fourth stage ends with the unveiling of the tombstone. On the death anniversary, according to the Jewish

✡ Throngs of religious Jews at the funeral of an outstanding and saintly rabbinic ✡ scholar.

calendar (called *Yahrzeit* in Yiddish), and during subsequent holy days when special memorial recitations take place, the former mourner rises again to recite the *kaddish*. While conducting the *Yahrzeit* for a relative, a male is often given the honour of leading the communal prayer. Sometimes an outsider may be hired to recite the *kaddish* for the deceased if, for some reason, the relatives are unable to do so. The prayers recited have an emotional and ritual significance; they include prayers for the "souls of the departed" so that the dead "find rest in the presence of the Almighty".

In this manner the dead are not "cut off" from the community. The memory of the dead is also kept alive by giving their names to newborns and by visiting their grave sites before *Rosh HaShanah* (also on the *Yahrzeit*). Past martyrs are remembered on Sabbath and holy days; graves of saints or sages often become pilgrimage sites where pilgrims pray for divine blessing through the intercession of this "righteous holy one" in Heaven. The graves of Rachel and the patriarchs in the Land of Israel are places of pilgrimage.

CHAPTER 6

Jewish Art

The crown of priesthood went to Aaron

(NUMBERS, 25:13)

The crown of kingship went to David

(PSALMS, 89:37)

But the crown of Torah *was set aside for whoever wishes to adorn himself with it.*
Lest you say, that this crown is inferior to the others—it is not so,
but rather superior to them and both depend on it.

(TALMUD YOMA, P. 72)

This is my G-d and I shall beautify Him. (EXODUS, 15:2)
How does one beautify G-d? By beautifying His *mitsvot* (TALMUD SHABBAT, P. 133)
Art was seen by Judaism as a vital part of life
Enhancing it and having a
Moral content.
The function of art in the
Jewish tradition is to
Elevate and ennoble man.

ו Judaism, as an entirely G-d-oriented and G-d-directed way of life encompasses the totality of the life of the individual. Every act in life and every decision must be directed toward spiritual elevation to a state of holiness and godliness as outlined in the *Torah*. This principle has traditionally determined Judaism's attitude towards art too. Recognising the human need for visual images in faith, Judaism does not suppress art, but circumscribes it.

Ritual Art

The Tabernacle in the wilderness and the ritual objects were the forerunners of the objects of Jewish ceremonial art which were to surround the Jew in his home and synagogue in later generations.

The **menorah**, the seven-branched candlebra which was destined to become a widely used emblem of Judaism, the table with the shewbread (twelve loaves displayed in a Jewish temple and renewed each Sabbath), the hangings and the altar—all these were functional ritual objects which also served as visible religious symbols for inspiration and spiritual elevation.

"This is my G-d and I shall glorify (by lighting, adorning or beautifying) Him," sings Moses. The *Talmud* explains that one adorns G-d with *mitsvot* (commandments): that the Jew is required to design, create and use beautiful, artistic ceremonial objects in fulfilling the commandments. The *Talmud* then goes on to list some of the ceremonial objects which should be created in a beautiful manner.

Artistic activity was encouraged, provided that it did not lead to idolatry or impair the unsullied belief in an omnipresent creator.

At each stage of their history, the Jews and their ancestors of biblical times expressed themselves in various art forms which inevitably reflected contemporary styles and fashions and the environment in which they lived. Jews have constantly produced or made use of objects which appeal in some fashion to their aesthetic senses for religious observance as well as for household and personal adornment.

✡ **Page 80**: The *menorah* is a seven-branched candlebra and is a widely used emblem of Judaism. **Below:** Hebrew manuscripts are illuminated in European style and ✡ technique.

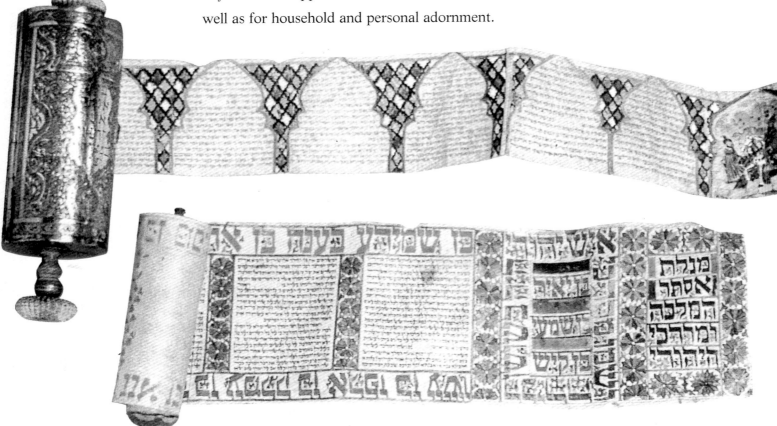

Hebrew **manuscripts** illuminated in the conventional sense in accordance with European styles and techniques began to emerge in Northern Europe not later than the 13th century. The *Sarajevo Haggadah* is the best known example of an illuminated manuscript.

It has already been mentioned that the *Talmud* has a general injunction that the glorification of G-d implies the use of the finest appurtenances in divine worship.

During the middle ages, it became an established practice to create objects specifically for every form of ritual use, thus emphasising the "glorification of the *mitsvah*". The favourite objects of Jewish ritual art were the **Torah**

ornaments, *kiddush* cups, *seder* plates, Sabbath lamps and spice boxes for the *havdalah* ceremony on the conclusion of the Sabbath. Heavily embroidered brocades with elaborate decorative inscriptions in gold were used both in the synagogues for the Ark curtains, or for the wrappings of the *Torah* scrolls, and in the home for Sabbath appurtenances and the like.

Historically, the *menorah* was the most important Jewish symbol, artistic emblem and ornamental device most frequently found in ancient times. It was so extensively used in antiquity that the *menorah* became the hallmark of Judaism, the single most distinctive, immediately identifiable emblem of Judaism throughout ancient Israel and elsewhere. It is also used extensively in Jewish funerary art and on Jewish gold glasses, coins, seals and amulets. It is presumably the Temple *menorah* that is depicted on the triumphal Arch of Titus in Rome—the *menorah* being carried by Jewish prisoners who were exiled from Israel, following the Roman victory over the Jews in 70 CE.

The kindling of the "*menorah* in the home" (the Sabbath lamp) is the central ritual for the inauguration of the Sabbath, for in this simple ceremony, the primary symbolic elements of Judaism are concentrated. Candlesticks and candelabra are used extensively for lighting the Sabbath lights. Several notable silver Sabbath lamps have been produced, each bearing designs of Jewish ceremonial art associated with the Sabbath, festivals of the Jewish year and other decorative motifs.

On Sabbath, the custom is to place the Sabbath breads on a special *challah* tray. The tray is, in turn, placed on a special **Sabbath tablecloth**.

✡
The *seder* plate used during the Passover festival, contains the symbolic food eaten at the festival, as well as the unleavened bread too at times. Decorated *seder* plates are also used.
✡

The *kiddush* ceremony ("sanctification") is an ancient ritual, and **the *kiddush* cup** is, therefore, one of the oldest Jewish ritual objects. It features Jewish symbols such as the *menorah* and *Shofar* and has Hebrew inscriptions, bearing portions of *kiddush* benedictions.

The **spice container,** a specifically Jewish ceremonial object used at the end of the Sabbath service, became very popular and was found in every Ashkenazic Jewish home. Its design was taken up by Jewish craftsmen and artists who, with a wealth of imaginative creativity, produced spice boxes of many materials and in a greater variety of forms than existed for any other Jewish ceremonial art.

Another example of Jewish decorative art in the home is the *mezuzah*. *Mezuzah* containers were designed usually of silver, brass or wood. These were at all times attractively decorated with a scene of the Holy Land.

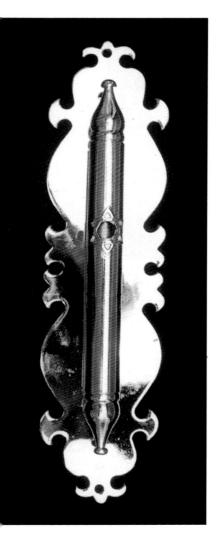

The *mezuzah* is found on the doorposts of every Jewish home.

Within the synagogue, the central sacred position was reserved for the *Torah,* the first five books of the Bible. Sumptuously adorned on Sabbaths and festivals, each *Torah* was dressed in colourful silks and brocades, with a silver breastplate and a *Torah* sceptre hanging over it and was surrounded by a regal crown of silver or a pair of tall silver finials with bells. All these artistic accessories were designed to draw attention to the majesty of the *Torah* and to give it a regal splendour.

The *Torah* scrolls were housed in the Holy Ark. By the sixteenth and seventeenth centuries, artistic craftsmanship centred around the *Torah* Ark had begun to produce majestic arks of exceptional beauty in sculptured and gilded wood, brass and silver.

A major appurtenance of the *Torah* Ark was the *Torah* curtain made from precious material such as coloured silk, velvet or velvet brocade, or different fine cloths richly embroidered with gold and silver threads. The embroidered designs included Jewish symbols like the crown of *Torah*, the Tablets of Law and the twin Temple columns.

The ***Ner Tamid*** (perpetual lamp) which hangs just above the Holy Ark, is kept alight day and night throughout the days of the year and symbolises the incessant and undying faith of the Jewish people.

The Prophet Elijah was the personification of absolute faith. Having complained to G-d that Israel had forsaken the ritual of circumcision (I Kings, 19:10,14), Elijah was ordered to witness the loyalty of Israel by being present at every circumcision ceremony. Referred to as "Angel of the covenant and protector of children", Elijah is said to be the invisible participant at circumcisions. Hence, before circumcision, the child is placed on the chair of Elijah. The Bene Israel of India designed different **chandeliers** to house the perpetual light; chairs carved out of wood for the Prophet Elijah and for the ceremony of circumcision were generally placed in all the synagogues in India.

During Hanukah, the Festival of Lights, the primary observance is the kindling of the Hanukah lamp called *Hanukiah*.

The *Hanukiah* is one of the most distinctive ceremonial objects and is found in most Jewish homes; many styles have been developed over the years. In Baghdad, several examples of *Hanukiot* featuring the motif of the oriental open-hand symbol were found. Circular and semi-circular *Hanukiot* have been found in India. The Jews of Bombay developed a style of *Hanukiah* in brass, often mounted on a wooden back. Popular designs for the back were the Magen David and a shield. They were designed in the form of removable rings which held large glasses filled with water and oil, and which were suspended on brass arms which fitted into brass grooves attached to the rear wall.

The **ketubah** (plural *ketubot*) is a written document that is an essential prerequisite to Jewish marriage. Being much more than a legal instrument, it is an informative historical and genealogical document that sheds a great deal of light on the social, religious, cultural and economic life of Jewish communities and mirrors vital segments of Jewish folk customs and practices. The *ketubot* of the Bene Israel of India are often full of colour, harmonised in a tasteful manner. They are characterised by a compartmentalisation of the basic *ketubah* text at the lower portion of the *ketubah*, which is surrounded by decoration, and of scriptural quotations of good wishes to the bride and groom, similarly surrounded at the upper portion. Flowers are frequently used as decoration. Columns representing the columns of the Jerusalem Temple also appear. The **Magen David** is an important symbol of the Bene Israel *ketubot*, and it continues to decorate most of their ceremonial art and their synagogues.

Jewish art expresses itself in architecture, religious objects and manuscripts.

Jewish art also expresses itself vividly through the architectural construction of synagogues, and in the manner of decoration as well as in their imposing appearance; early funerary Art; the written and printed word, consisting of illuminated Hebrew manuscripts and decorated books; Jewish paintings and sculptures, ceremonial art, festivals and rituals.

MAIMONIDES' PRINCIPLES
The Fundamentals of Jewish Faith

י״ג עקרים של הרמב״ם

CHAPTER 7

More Teachings, More Beliefs

Anyone who gives charity to a poor person in a surly manner and with a gloomy face completely nullifies the merit of his own deed, even if he gives while sympathising with him who is in trouble, as it is written: "Did I not weep for him whose day was hard? Was not my soul grieved for the poor?"

(JOB, 30:25).

He should speak to him graciously and comfortingly, as it is written, "I gladdened the heart of the widow."

(JOB, 29:13)

Let not the repentant person imagine that he is far removed from the merit of the righteous on account of the iniquities and sins he has committed. He is tenderly loved by the Creator as if he had never sinned. The sages said: "Where repentant sinners stand the thoroughly Righteous cannot stand."

(TALMUD BERACHOT, P. 34)

Among the first things that the Bible tells us about Adam is that he was created in the image of G-d (Genesis, 1:27). A non-Jewish religious teacher interpreted the above statement to mean that G-d has a body and that the human form is created in the image of G-d's body. Jewish teachings maintain, however, that G-d is incorporeal, without a body (Deuteronomy, 4:12-15). Animals do not have the reasoning power to make moral choices. Human beings are the only creatures who do. It is in this regard that human beings are considered to be in G-d's image.

Man is Free

All religious sources in Judaism—the Bible, the prayer book, the *Talmud*, the rabbis and philosophers are unanimous on the matter concerning freedom of man. They all maintain that man is free to choose whichever path he wishes to follow—the good or the bad. Even when circumstances are against him, it is his duty to rise above them and choose the good. Man is therefore free and he is completely responsible for what path he chooses for himself.

Born without Sin

The Jewish people believe that man's soul is pure. During the journey of life, he may, undoubtedly, be exposed to great temptations and show an inclination to sin. Judaism does not accept that man is born with the inheritance of the original sin transmitted to him from the first man, Adam. Man may have the inclination to sin but this does not mean that he is destined to sin. Furthermore, although a man may have the tendency to sin, he is possessed of the power to rid himself of sin.

Life after Death

The Jewish religion definitely believes in some form of eternal life. Man is born from eternity and after death, goes back to the same eternal source. His life is not limited by the boundaries of earthly existence. Beyond the beginning and beyond the end, there is the nearness of G-d, the eternal source and eternal end. Judaism lays stress upon the spiritual and godlike characteristics in man. It maintains that the spiritual or soul element is exalted above death and is the cornerstone of life. Even beyond death, the life of the soul remains. Belief in this teaching of Judaism brings peace and added meaning to life on earth. The Jewish belief in life after death and the immortality of the soul has always been an inherent part of Jewish religious thought and is among the cardinal principals of the faith. The spark of the divine spirit, the *neshamah*, shows that the soul of man is immortal and not confined within the perimeters of time. It belongs to the infinite in the sense that it returns to its divine Creator. With this deep-seated belief in the immortality of the soul, the authoritative teaching of Judaism warns man not to speculate unnecessarily about the details of life after death.

Unity of God: Intrinsic to All Religions

To the Jew, Judaism is the true faith. Judaism teaches that G-d's reward is not reserved only for the good Jew but is promised to the righteous of all nations.

The rabbis believed that "the righteous of the nations of the world have a portion in the world to come" (Tosefta Sanhedrin, 13:2). They had high regard for righteous non-Jews and even held them up on occasion as moral exemplars. Whereas Judaism binds Jews by the 613 laws of the *Torah*, it demands fulfillment only of the Seven Noahide Laws from non-Jews.

Judaism teaches that G-d's love is extended to all His creatures—Jews and the non-Jews—and that there is no monopoly of salvation to those who possess a certain faith. The hope of Judaism is not bound up with the idea that all mankind will become Jews and observe the law, but rather centred in the idea that the truth of the one G-d and the brotherhood of man will be realised by all mankind and become the guiding force in the practical life of all.

The Messiah: The Lord's Anointed One

One of the final principles of the Jewish faith as enumerated by the great medieval Jewish thinker, Maimonides, reads as follows:

> "I believe with a perfect faith in the coming of the 'Messiah',
> and, though he tarry, I will wait daily for his coming."

The Hebrew word for Messiah—*Mashiach*—literally means "anointed" and was the term often used for a Jewish king or a High Priest, both of whom were anointed with oil as a part of their ceremony of induction.

When David received the divine promise that the throne would remain in his family forever (II Samuel, 7:13), the title acquired a special reference and signified the representative of the royal line of David. The prophetic vision of the eventual establishment of divine kingship on earth came to be identified with the restoration of Israel under the leadership of the Messiah, the L-rd's anointed.

The traditional outlook of Judaism is that the Messiah will be the dominating figure in an age of universal peace and plenty; through restored Israel, he will bring about the spiritual regeneration of humanity, when all will blend into one brotherhood to perform righteousness with a perfect heart. "On that day the L-rd shall be One and his name One." (Zechariah, 14:9). Jewish prayers are replete with references to the Messianic hopes and aspirations. There is hardly a prophet of note who does not mention the Messiah and the Messianic age.

The prophetic view is that nature itself will be transformed in the Messianic days, when the power of death will be limited. In the golden age of humanity, there will be a return to longevity, and those who die at a hundred will be reckoned as but children, prematurely cut off for their sins. "No sound of weeping, no voice of crying shall ever be heard in it; no child shall die there anymore in infancy, nor any old man who has not lived out his years of life; he who dies youngest lives a hundred years . . ." (Isaiah, 65:19-20).

The signs heralding the advent of the Messiah at the end of the time of captivity are described in the Mishnah Sotah (9:15) in such terms as these: "With the footprints of Messiah, insolence will increase . . . the vine will yield its fruit but the wine will be costly . . . scholarships will degenerate, piety will be rejected, and truth will nowhere be found; youth will be impudent . . . and a man's enemies will be the members of his own household."

A *midrashic* statement says that three days before the advent of the Messiah, Elijah would appear on the mountains of Israel and exclaim: "O mountains of Israel, how long will you remain waste and desolate!" Then he would proclaim world peace, and G-d would redeem Israel. (Pesikta Rabbathi, 35)

In *Malachi*, 3:23-24, Elijah is introduced as a type for all times, occupying a prominent place in Jewish lore as the prophet who "will turn the hearts of fathers to their children and the hearts of children to their fathers" before the coming of the great day of the L-rd. This has led to Elijah being described in Jewish tradition as the forerunner of the Messiah.

Since the Messiah may appear at any time and from any parentage, Elijah's name is associated with every circumcision, celebration or birth *(milah)*. The invisible presence of Elijah at the *seder* celebration is derived from the idea of the Passover of the Future as contrasted with the Passover of Egypt.

There is a Talmudic statement which reads: "Blasted be the bones of those who calculate the end, for when the calculated time comes and the Messiah does not appear, people despair of his ever coming." (Talmud Sanhedrin, p. 97). Hence, Maimonides writes: "All these matters concerning the coming of the Messiah will not be known to anyone until they happen . . . In the Messianic days there will be no hunger or war, no jealousy or strife; prosperity will be universal, and the world's predominant occupation will be to know the L-rd." (Yad, Melakhim, 12:2,5). This is based on the prophesy which envisions the eradication of evil from human society and a corresponding regeneration of the rest of creation: "Then the wolf shall live with the lamb, and the leopard shall lie down with the kid . . . ." (Isaiah, 11:6-9)

Maimonides envisaged the Messianic era as a "natural" time in which nearly all the physical laws of the universe would be maintained; nonetheless it would not be totally devoid of supernatural occurrences. Thus, there would be a resurrection of the dead,

✡ "If there be no quarrelling among men, G-d's judgement does not touch them." (Zohor, vol. 1, p. 76) ✡

whose bodies and souls would be reunited for a limited period of time. Essentially, this era would introduce a period of complete social justice.

The Messiah would concern himself not only with the ingathering of the exiles from the four corners of the earth to the Holy Land, but also with international harmony and peace and with the promotion of humanity's acceptance of G-d as the sole ruler of the universe.

Praying and hoping for the Messiah is the most cherished dream of every Jew, who, in true Jewish spirit, prays for the establishment of the kingdom of G-d on earth. The term "kingdom of G-d" does not refer to a "land" which will descend upon earth from some other world, nor does it mean the divine pattern of life after death. The kingdom of G-d is the world of man as it should be in the eyes of G-d—the ideal world in which man will ensure that there is no evil (in accordance with the teaching of G-d). In a broader

perspective, it refers to an ideal world—not for Jews alone, but for all nations. This philosophy best describes the universalistic teachings of Judaism.

This same philosophy finds classical expression in the prophecies of Isaiah and Micah: "And it shall come to pass in the end of days that the mountain of the L-rd's house shall be established on the top of the mountains, and shall be exalted above the hills, and all nations shall flow unto it. And many peoples shall go and say: 'Come ye and let us go up to the mountain of the L-rd, to the house of the G-d of Jacob and He will teach us of His ways and we will walk in His paths, for out of Zion will go forth the law and the word of the L-rd from Jerusalem.' And He shall judge between nations, and shall decide for many people; and they shall beat their swords into ploughshares, and their spears into pruning hooks; nation shall not lift up sword against nation, neither shall they learn wars any more." (Isaiah, 2:2-4)

From the Universal to the Particular

On the one hand, Judaism maintains specific duties for Jews; on the other, it maintains the ideal of the universal brotherhood of man and that it is a faith that preaches G-d's salvation to the righteous of all nations and creeds. How are both these opposing ideas to be reconciled? The fact is that they are not really opposing ideas at all. It is well recognised that the individual is a member of his family as well as of the community. In the first, he develops himself fully to be able to take his proper place in the wider community.

In the same way, a Jew is first a member of his own community with its distinctive laws, customs and culture. After developing himself to his full potential, he is best fitted to play his part as a member of the wider brotherhood of man.

In Judaism there is room for both particularism and universalism, with no rivalry between them at all. Religion and morality blend into an indissoluble unity. The love of G-d is incomplete without the love of one's fellowmen. The goals towards which this concept leads are the elimination of man-made misery and suffering, prejudice and strife, tyranny and social inequality. Judaism champions the cause of universal peace, (the ideal proclaimed to mankind from the days of the prophets) and abhors all violence. It emphasises the kinship of the human race and the sanctity of human life and freedom.

Judaism is thus the special religion of a separate people, but the people and the faith are dedicated to the most comprehensive and universal ideals.

The Concise Timeline of Jewish History

BEFORE THE COMMON ERA

1800: The covenant between G-d and Abraham; the beginning of Judaism.

1250: The Exodus; Moses leads the children of Israel out of Egyptian slavery.

The revelation at Mount Sinai

G-d gives His commandments to the children of Israel.

1200: The conquest of Canaan; Joshua leads the Israelis into the Promised Land.

1030: The period of the Judges

The Tribes settle down; unrest and strife; attacks from surrounding nations; civil rule of a succession of judges; Saul anointed king; the establishment of the monarchy.

950: The Holy Temple is built

Worship of G-d in the magnificent Temple in Jerusalem; political and religious unity.

931: Split of the Kingdom

After Solomon's death, the United Kingdom split into two: ten tribes led by Jeroboam and two tribes of Judah led by Rechoboam.

750 to 450: The Age of the Latter Prophets

G-d's message of obedience to the commandments and social justice; punishment for transgression; repentance, forgiveness and restoration—all taught by the prophets.

722: The Assyrian defeat of the Kingdom of Israel

Kingdom of Israel destroyed; result—"ten lost tribes"; only Judah remains.

586: The fall of Jerusalem, destruction of the Holy Temple and the Exile

Land overrun by Babylonians; end of sacrificial worship at the Holy Temple, political independence and sovereignty. Jewish existence without the Holy Temple; beginning of the formulation of prayers; Jewish existence as inhabitants in a host country.

538: King Cyrus of Persia grants permission to return to the Land of Israel

Persia defeats Babylonia and permits the Jewish people to return to Israel.

520: The rebuilding of the Holy Temple

Sacrificial worship in the centralised sanctuary in Jerusalem resumes.

THE COMMON ERA

70: The fall of Jerusalem

Destruction of the Second Holy Temple and the exile; land overrun by Romans.

600: The Babylonian *Talmud* is completed

Exiled sages (in Babylonia) extend the Oral Law of the *Mishnah* and *Gemara*.

The Middle Ages

Continued development of Jewish Law and theology; beginning of the *kabbalah*, the mystical tradition; "Golden Age" in Spain; publication of *Shulkhan Arukh*.

Mid 1700s: The development of Chassidism and the major Yeshivot (theological seminaries)

1938-1945: The Holocaust

1948: The modern State of Israel is established

Pages 94-95: "Let us go up to the mountain of the L-rd, to the house of the G-d of Jacob and He will teach us of His ways and we will walk in His paths, for out of Zion will go forth the law and the word of the L-rd from Jerusalem." (Isaiah, 2:3)

PHOTO CREDITS

Amit Pasricha: Pages 1, 17, 43 (top), 50 (top), 51

Board of Jewish Education, Inc.: Pages 37, 38 (top)

Consulate General of Israel in New York: Pages 4, 82

The Israeli Embassy, New Delhi: Pages 22, 27, 32, 33, 42, 43 (bottom),
47, 50 (bottom), 56, 58, (top), 68, 73, 74, 75, 78-79, 80, 88, 94-95

Ghigo Roli: Pages 10, 62, 71

Hannah Satz: Pages 2, 21, 28-29, 30, 55, 66, 91

Marcello Bertinetti: Pages 8-9, 18, 20, 25 (top), 26, 48, 50 (top), 51, 61

Tifereth Israel Synagogue, Jacob Circle, Mumbai: Page 16

ASAP

Beth Hatefutsoth: Page 24

Israel Talby: Pages 34, 38 (bottom), 52, 53, 54, 58 (bottom), 76

Itzik Marom: Page 57

Jacob Kaszemacher: Pages 62, 72

Joel Fishman: Page 83

Rafi Magnes: Page 39 (top)

Richard Nowitz: Page 39 (bottom)

EIKONOS

Keith Glasgow: Page 44

M. Ravenna: Page 23